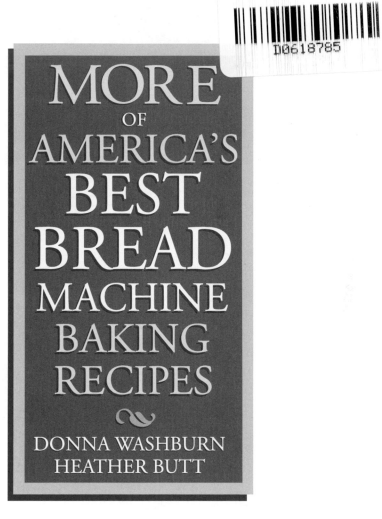

MORE
OF
AMERICA'S
BEST
BREAD
MACHINE
BAKING
RECIPES

DONNA WASHBURN
HEATHER BUTT

Robert
ROSE

More of America's Best Bread Machine Baking Recipes

For complete cataloguing data, see page 4.

Cover photo: wedges of PUMPERNICKEL TURBAN *(page 140)*

DESIGN, EDITORIAL AND PRODUCTION:	MATTHEWS COMMUNICATIONS DESIGN INC.
PHOTOGRAPHY:	MARK T. SHAPIRO
ART DIRECTION, FOOD PHOTOGRAPHY:	SHARON MATTHEWS
FOOD STYLIST:	KATE BUSH
PROP STYLIST:	CHARLENE ERRICSON
MANAGING EDITOR:	PETER MATTHEWS
INDEX:	BARBARA SCHON
COLOR SCANS & FILM:	PointOne GRAPHICS

We acknowledge the financial support of the Government of Canada through the Book Publishing Industry Development Program (BPIDP) for our publishing activities.

Published by: Robert Rose Inc. • 120 Eglinton Ave. E., Suite 1000
Toronto, Ontario, Canada M4P 1E2 Tel: (416) 322-6552

Printed in Canada
1234567 BP 03 02 01 00

CONTENTS

INTRODUCTION 7

FLAVORS BY REQUEST 11

HEALTHY AND HEARTY GRAINS 27

FLAVORFUL FILLED AND FLATBREADS 41

MORE FROM THE HEARTH 57

SEEDS AND NUTS 71

MORE BAGELS AND SOURDOUGHS 83

SWEET DOUGHS AND LOAVES 95

INTERNATIONAL BREADS 113

SHAPES FOR EVERY OCCASION 129
(FOR THE KID IN YOU)

GLUTEN-FREE AND OTHER SPECIAL 149
DIETARY BREADS

BEYOND BREADS 163

EQUIPMENT GLOSSARY 176

INGREDIENT GLOSSARY 177

TECHNIQUES GLOSSARY 183

INDEX 185

Canadian Cataloguing in Publication Data

Washburn, Donna
  More of America's best bread machine baking recipes

Includes index.
ISBN 0-7788-0021-0

1. Bread. 2. Automatic bread machines. 3. Cookery (Bread). I. Butt, Heather. II. Title.

TX769.W37 2000   641.8'15   C00-931305-2

To our husbands

David and Jack

and our sons

Jeff, Stephen, Ian and Craig

Acknowledgements

We would like to thank everyone who has helped to make this book a reality. Without their assistance, the recipes would still be ideas in our heads.

Thank you to all the manufacturers — Panasonic, Philips Electronics, Proctor-Silex, Regal, Sunbeam/Oster, Toastmaster, West Bend, Black & Decker, Philips Norelco and Zojirushi — who supplied the machines used in testing. To our lifeline at Philips Electronics, Jean Hill, a special thanks for your continuing support and assistance.

We would also like to thank the individuals and companies who kindly supplied product to the test kitchen. For yeast and flour, thanks to Nathalie Radepont and Jim Kopp of fermipan® yeast from Lallemand Inc., and to Glenna Vance of Red Star Yeast & Products and to Sarah Prunk and Shannon Zappala of King Arthur Flour. Also to Bruce Wright of The Brewing Experience, thank you for providing malt syrup. And to Brian Creighton of Myer's Bulk Foods, our appreciation for filling our orders and serving as an ongoing source of product information. To Linda Williams and staff of New Horizons Foods, thank you for all your help. A special thanks goes to Carol Coulter, our favorite celiac, for her assistance with the gluten-free recipes.

We have always believed that photography is an important part of cookbooks. And we have once again been fortunate to work with a very talented group of people who make our breads look so appealing: Mark Shapiro, of Mark Shapiro Photography; food stylist Kate Bush; art director Sharon Matthews; and prop stylist Charlene Ericson. Thank you to all for your untiring efforts and ability to work miracles.

Special thanks go to our publisher, Bob Dees and the staff of Robert Rose Inc. Also to Peter Matthews and the staff of Matthews Communications Design Inc. for working through all the intricacies of editorial, design, layout and production. Thank you to Pat Morris for recipe testing. And thanks for editing this book, Peter; we enjoyed working with you.

Last but by no means least, we want to thank the people who are always there for us (even when we're not writing cookbooks) — our husbands, for their support, words of wisdom and unbiased (of course) taste testing. A special thank you to our sons and all the members of our extended families for the assistance they have supplied with their individual expertise.

After all the work producing our second cookbook, you might think we would be getting a little tired of bread. But you'd be wrong, because the fragrance of baked bread still warms our hearts. We hope you have as many enjoyable hours baking the recipes in this cookbook as we have had developing them for you.

Introduction

Not long after we received the freshly printed copies of our first cookbook, *America's Best Bread Machine Baking Recipes*, our publisher called to tell us that he thought we had a runaway bestseller on our hands. And he was right — over 40,000 books sold in the first nine months. Amazing! Our deepest thanks and appreciation to everyone who purchased a book, especially to those who contacted our publisher with kind words about our recipes.

This past year has been a busy one in the test kitchen of Quality Professional Services, our recipe development company. Well over 30 machines continued to knead, proof and bake bread daily. We continued to visit bakeries, grocery stores and restaurants — and, of course, sample breads. We keep up with the latest ingredients and food trends so we can bring you recipes to complement any meal.

Immediately after our first book went to press, Philips Electronics Ltd. asked QPS to develop recipes for the manuals of their two new horizontal bread machines. What a challenge! These machines have many new features and cycles including: Cake, Jam, Quick Bread, Rapid One-Hour Basic, Rapid Whole Wheat and Pasta. They bake two or three sizes of loaves with a choice of three crust colors.

As the Home Economists for Philips Electronics Ltd., and as the test kitchen experts for fermipan® yeast from Lallemand Inc., we speak with many of you while managing the call center and answering toll-free customer service calls. We thoroughly enjoy helping answer your questions. We love the challenge of not knowing what difficulty or what interesting bit of information the next caller may have to offer. This year, as spokespersons for Robin Hood Multifood's bread flours, we have had the opportunity to promote bread machine baking on TV.

When asked by our publisher, Bob Dees, president of Robert Rose Inc., we readily agreed to author a second bread machine cookbook. Once again the writing of a book has allowed two very good friends to work together bringing you new recipes.

We also publish a bimonthly 12-page newsletter for bread machine owners — called *The Bread Basket* — which features new recipes, bread machine reviews and lots of tips and techniques. Turn to the back of the book and you'll find more information about this newsletter as well as a subscription form.

Our newsletter subscribers tell us they can never get enough bread machine recipes. And we often get requests for particular flavor combinations that come from recipes belonging to our readers' mothers or grandmothers. Many have special memories attached to holidays and family celebrations. We have adapted these to the bread machine and have included many of these flavor requests in the first chapter of this book.

We hope you'll enjoy this wonderful collection of recipes. We've created them just for you — our fellow bread-machine bakers.

Donna and Heather

About the Recipes

There are many challenges in developing bread machine recipes. And one of the greatest is keeping up with changes in bread machines themselves. Just a few years ago, for example, most bread machines were of the "vertical" type, producing a tall loaf with a square slice. Today, the majority of machines sold are horizontal-style, producing a loaf that has a round top and looks like a traditional slice. In addition, some models bake hotter than others, some knead longer, some preheat before mixing and some have longer rising periods. Today's bread machines also have numerous new cycles, up to a maximum of 14, and most make more than one size of loaf with several crust settings. Some bake one size better than another.

Since the same recipe can look quite different in these various types of machine, we have tested each recipe in this book using a minimum of three different brands and models of both horizontal and vertical style. The recipe is then adjusted and retested until it produces the best possible loaf in all three machines.

ADJUSTING THE RECIPES

Given the variances between different types of machines (and your individual preferences), you may wish to adjust the recipe. We recommend that you first try the recipe as given. If the loaf is a bit compact and short, increase the yeast by 1/4 to 1/2 tsp (1 to 2 mL). On the other hand, if it mushrooms over the edges of the baking pan and hits the top, increase the flour slightly and decrease the yeast by 1/4 to 1/2 tsp (1 to 2 mL).

Each recipe is developed to have a texture and flavor of its own. For example, the HAWAIIAN SUNRISE (see recipe, page 109), is similar to an angel food cake in its lightness and fluffiness, while the SWISS RYE (see recipe, page 128) is heavier, with a fine texture. The consistency of dough balls also varies. Sweet bread dough must be softer than most bread dough or dried or candied fruit won't mix in, but just sit on the outside and burn. Recipes containing oatmeal are thinner in the beginning but thicken during kneading, resulting in fine-textured loaves. Resist the urge to adjust the dough ball or all of your loaves will have the same texture.

LOAF SIZE

You will notice an "**L**" beside some of the 2 lb (1 kg) recipes. This indicates an extra large loaf. If your bread pan has a capacity of less than 12 cups (3 L) (see chart, below), try the smaller-size recipe first. These recipes work well in some of the new horizontal two-paddle machines, which are advertised by the manufacturers as 2.5 lb (1.25 kg) machines.

HOW BIG IS YOUR BAKING PAN?

Determine the volume of your baking pan by filling it with water, using a measuring cup. Consult the chart below to verify the size of recipe to use.

BREAD MACHINE SIZES AND CAPACITIES		
Loaf size	Weight	Capacity of baking pan
Medium	1.5 lb (750 g)	6 to 9 cups (1.5 to 2.25 L)
Large	2 lb (1 kg)	9 to 12 cups (2.25 to 3 L)
Extra Large	2.5 lb (1.25 kg)	12 to 16 cups (3 to 4 L)

TEMPERATURE OF INGREDIENTS

The success of bread machine baking often depends on having ingredients at the right temperature. Loaves rise higher with a lighter texture if *milk, vegetable juices* and *fruit juices* are at room temperature. (To warm approximately 1 cup [250 mL] liquid to room temperature, microwave on High for 1 minute.) Mixtures such as *pumpkin, yams, squash, applesauce, pears* and *mashed banana* should be at room temperature before using. Use *eggs* straight from the refrigerator unless specified otherwise in the recipe.

Cream cheese and *butter* should be softened.

TESTING FOR DONENESS

There are two methods. The most common is to tap on the bottom and if the sound is hollow, the bread is baked. If you have an instant-read thermometer, insert into bread at least 2 inches (5 cm). The thermometer should register 190° F (93° C).

The Bread Machine Pantry

Great bread depends on choosing the correct ingredients and measuring them accurately. Let's consider the most common ingredients (see Ingredient Glossary, page 177, for more information).

• Flour

Flour contains *gluten*, a protein that traps the gas bubbles and air, which causes the dough to rise.

Unbleached or bleached, bread flour give similar baking results. However, cake-and-pastry flour or self-rising blends are not suitable to bake bread.

Enrichment is the process that adds back to the flour the vitamins and minerals removed during the refining process. Most of the vitamins and minerals are found in the bran and germ. The bran in whole wheat flour supplies the fiber.

Both wheat and rye flours contain gluten, although rye flour has less, and must be used in combination with wheat flour in bread machine baking. Be careful when working with rye flour, since the gluten in it is not very elastic and becomes sticky with over-kneading. We do not recommend exceeding the amounts of rye flour given for any of the recipes in this book.

To preserve its "strength" (ability to rise), store all flour in an airtight container in a cool, dry place. Do not store flour in the refrigerator, where it can pick up moisture. Flour should be frozen for storage of longer than 6 months. Allow the flour to return to room temperature before using.

• Liquids

Water yields a crisper crust, while *milk* supplies some fat to bake a softer, more tender loaf.

Use whatever type of milk you prefer: homogenized, 2%, 1%, low-fat or skim. When using the timer on your machine, use nonfat dry milk or buttermilk powder. In recipes that specify powdered milk (where you won't be using the timer), you can use fluid milk to replace the water and omit the powder.

Fruit juice intensifies flavor and color. Purchase unsweetened fruit juices for consistent results. The amount of sugar and salt varies in juices. Read the label to be sure the product you purchase is a fruit juice and not a "fruit drink."

• Salt

While we have used only small amounts of salt in our recipes, the salt is necessary, since it controls the yeast's activity, and prevents the loaf from over-rising and collapsing. Breads made without salt are very bland and over-risen.

• Yeast

Yeast converts the carbohydrates in flour and sugar to produce the carbon dioxide gas that causes dough to rise. Bread machine yeast and instant yeast are both very active types, and can be added directly to the bread machine without the need for pre-activating. Our recipes were developed using bread machine yeast.

The "expiry date" on the package means that it should be opened before that date and used within a 2-month period. Store a 2- to 3-month supply of yeast in an airtight container in the refrigerator. For long-term storage, yeast should be kept in an airtight container in the freezer.

Do not transfer yeast from one container to another; exposing it to air can shorten its life.

The amount of yeast used in large- and small-loaf versions of each recipe is specific to that recipe; it is not simply factored up or down according to size. In fact, for some recipes, the amount of yeast in the 2 lb (1 kg) version is the same as (or even *smaller* than) the amount of yeast used in the 1.5 lb (750 g) version.

• Sugars

Sugar, honey, maple syrup, corn syrup and molasses can be used interchangeably. Results vary slightly in color, flavor and texture.

Aspartame-based sugar substitutes can be used, but not those based on saccharin. Substitute equal amounts for the sugar in the recipe. Loaves are lighter in color than when sugar is used.

• Fats

Fat gives the crust its tenderness and the loaf its softness. It also helps to retain moisture, which keeps the loaf from going stale too quickly. The type of fat used is a matter of preference — and can include shortening, margarine, butter or vegetable oil. (Your choice may have some effect on the loaf, however.) Do not use low-calorie margarine since its high water content will affect the size and texture of the loaf.

Cheese and egg yolk contribute to the fat in some recipes. Use large eggs directly from the refrigerator. When measuring shredded cheese, do not pack. Weight is a more accurate measure than volume.

FLAVORS BY REQUEST

TIPS FOR TERRIFIC LOAVES	12
APPLE YAM LOAF	13
ASIAGO HERB LOAF	14
CALIFORNIA GARLIC WITH SUN-DRIED TOMATOES	15
CARROT PINEAPPLE BREAD	16
CHEESY POTATO LOAF	17
CHRISTINE'S FRUITED PUMPERNICKEL	18
CINNAMON APPLE OAT	20
ENGLISH MUFFIN LOAF	21
MALTED RYE BREAD	22
MUSHROOM LEEK	23
PESTO LOAF	24
QUICK POULTRY-STUFFING LOAF	25
SAN FRANCISCO FIREHOUSE BREAD	26

We frequently hear from readers with ideas for new and interesting flavor combinations — often based on old, traditional bread recipes passed down from mothers and grandmothers. We've incorporated some of these ideas here. Perhaps you'll find a new family favorite of your own.

TIPS FOR TERRIFIC LOAVES

• Measure accurately. The bread machine is unforgiving!

• For a more tender loaf, use homogenized or 2% milk, or cultured buttermilk, instead of water and nonfat dry milk or buttermilk powder. Just add an amount equal to the water called for in the recipe.

• If using buttermilk powder, it should be added after the flour. Adding it directly to the water will cause lumps.

• Most loaves can be baked using the timer. Exceptions are those containing dairy products and other perishables such as eggs and meats.

• Use large-size eggs, cold from the refrigerator.

• Butter should be at room temperature and added in small dollops.

• Where cinnamon or garlic is used in a recipe, do not exceed the amount specified. These ingredients can inhibit the action of the yeast.

• For recipes that call for milk and large quantities of fruits and vegetables (such as sweet potatoes and applesauce) these ingredients should be warmed to room temperature before adding to the baking pan.

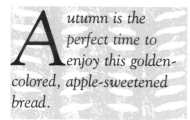

Autumn is the perfect time to enjoy this golden-colored, apple-sweetened bread.

Tip

One medium apple yields approximately 3/4 cup (175 mL) grated apple. No need to peel; just core, then grate or chop.

Variation

We tested this recipe with both Granny Smith and McIntosh apples, but you can try Spy, Cortland or your favorite regional baking apple.

Try substituting an equal amount of unsweetened applesauce for the apple.

Apple Yam Loaf

1.5 LB (750 G)

1/2 cup	unsweetened apple juice	125 mL
1/2 cup	canned yams, well-drained and chopped	125 mL
1	medium apple, grated or chopped	1
1 1/4 tsp	salt	6 mL
2 tbsp	butter	25 mL
3 3/4 cups	bread flour	925 mL
1 1/4 tsp	bread machine yeast	6 mL

2 LB (1 KG)   L

2/3 cup	unsweetened apple juice	150 mL
2/3 cup	canned yams, well-drained and chopped	150 mL
1	medium apple, grated or chopped	1
1 1/2 tsp	salt	7 mL
2 tbsp	butter	25 mL
4 cups	bread flour	1000 mL
1 3/4 tsp	bread machine yeast	7 mL

1. Measure ingredients into baking pan in the order recommended by the manufacturer. Insert pan into the oven chamber. Select **Sweet Cycle**.

The sweet aroma of this loaf baking will have you counting the minutes until you can slice it.

Tip

In all recipes calling for cheese, cut it into chunks or grate. Chunks will melt during baking.

For cheese weight/volume equivalents, see Ingredient Glossary (page 177).

If you have leftovers, this loaf makes the tastiest croutons. Sprinkle over a green or Caesar salad.

Asiago Herb Loaf

1.5 LB (750 G)

1 cup	water	250 mL
3/4 tsp	salt	4 mL
1 tbsp	granulated sugar	15 mL
3 1/4 cups	bread flour	800 mL
1/2 cup	Asiago cheese	125 mL
1 tsp	dried basil	5 mL
1 tsp	fennel seeds	5 mL
1 tsp	dried oregano	5 mL
1 1/4 tsp	bread machine yeast	5 mL

2 LB (1 KG)

1 1/3 cups	water	325 mL
1 tsp	salt	5 mL
1 tbsp	granulated sugar	15 mL
4 1/4 cups	bread flour	1050 mL
3/4 cup	Asiago cheese	175 mL
1 1/2 tsp	dried basil	7 mL
1 1/2 tsp	fennel seeds	7 mL
1 1/2 tsp	dried oregano	7 mL
1 1/2 tsp	bread machine yeast	6 mL

1. Measure ingredients into baking pan in the order recommended by the manufacturer. Insert pan into the oven chamber. Select **Sweet Cycle**.

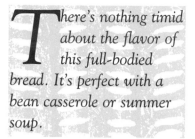

There's nothing timid about the flavor of this full-bodied bread. It's perfect with a bean casserole or summer soup.

Tip

For a richer tomato color, add the snipped, sun-dried tomatoes to the water.

Use dry (not oil-packed) sun-dried tomatoes.

See the Techniques Glossary (page 183) for instructions on roasting garlic.

Yes, you're reading it right: The 1.5 lb (750 g) recipe contains the *same* amount of yeast as the 2 lb (1 kg).

Variation

For stronger garlic flavor use fresh instead of roasted garlic.

California Garlic with Sun-Dried Tomatoes

1.5 LB (750 G)

1 1/2 cups	tomato vegetable juice (room temperature)	375 mL
1/3 cup	snipped sun-dried tomatoes	75 mL
3	cloves roasted garlic	3
1 1/2 tsp	salt	7 mL
2 tbsp	granulated sugar	25 mL
2 tbsp	olive oil	25 mL
3 3/4 cups	bread flour	925 mL
1 tbsp	dried basil	15 mL
1 3/4 tsp	bread machine yeast	8 mL

2 LB (1 KG)

1 3/4 cups	tomato vegetable juice (room temperature)	425 mL
1/2 cup	snipped sun-dried tomatoes	125 mL
4	cloves roasted garlic	4
1 3/4 tsp	salt	8 mL
3 tbsp	granulated sugar	45 mL
2 tbsp	olive oil	25 mL
4 1/4 cups	bread flour	1050 mL
2 tbsp	dried basil	25 mL
1 3/4 tsp	bread machine yeast	8 mL

1. Measure ingredients into baking pan in the order recommended by the manufacturer. Insert pan into the oven chamber. Select **Basic Cycle**.

Your child won't eat veggies? Spread this slightly sweet bread with peanut butter. You'll be asked for seconds.

Tip

Use unsweetened pineapple chunks packed in pineapple juice (not syrup). A 19-oz (540 mL) can contains approximately 2 cups (500 mL).

Yes, you're reading it right: The 1.5 lb (750 g) recipe contains *same* amount of yeast than the 2 lb (1 kg).

Variation

For an extra burst of flavor, add 1 to 2 tsp (5 to 10 mL) orange zest.

Carrot Pineapple Bread

1.5 LB (750 G)

1 cup	grated carrots	250 mL
1/2 cup	pineapple chunks, juice reserved	125 mL
1/2 cup	pineapple juice (drained from chunks)	125 mL
1/4 cup	nonfat dry milk	50 mL
1 1/4 tsp	salt	6 mL
3 tbsp	granulated sugar	45 mL
1 tbsp	vegetable oil	15 mL
3 cups	bread flour	750 mL
2 tsp	bread machine yeast	10 mL

2 LB (1 KG)   L

1 1/4 cups	grated carrots	300 mL
3/4 cup	pineapple chunks, juice reserved	175 mL
1/2 cup	pineapple juice (drained from chunks)	125 mL
1/3 cup	nonfat dry milk	75 mL
1 1/2 tsp	salt	7 mL
1/4 cup	granulated sugar	50 mL
2 tbsp	vegetable oil	25 mL
3 3/4 cups	bread flour	925 mL
2 tsp	bread machine yeast	10 mL

1. Measure ingredients into baking pan in the order recommended by the manufacturer. Insert pan into the oven chamber. Select **Basic Cycle**.

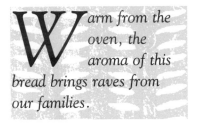

Warm from the oven, the aroma of this bread brings raves from our families.

Tip

For cheese weight/volume equivalents, see Ingredient Glossary (page 177).

Yes, you're reading it right: The 1.5 lb (750 g) recipe contains *same* amount of yeast than the 2 lb (1 kg).

Variation

Substitute Monterey Jack, Swiss, Parmesan, Romano (or a mixture of these cheeses) for the Cheddar.

Cheesy Potato Loaf

1.5 LB (750 G)

1 1/3 cups	water	325 mL
1/4 cup	nonfat dry milk	50 mL
1 1/4 tsp	salt	6 mL
2 tbsp	granulated sugar	25 mL
3 cups	bread flour	750 mL
1/3 cup	instant potato flakes	75 mL
3/4 cup	grated aged Cheddar cheese	175 mL
1/4 tsp	dry mustard	1 mL
1 1/4 tsp	bread machine yeast	6 mL

2 LB (1 KG)

1 2/3 cups	water	400 mL
1/3 cup	nonfat dry milk	75 mL
1 1/2 tsp	salt	7 mL
3 tbsp	granulated sugar	45 mL
3 1/2 cups	bread flour	875 mL
1/2 cup	instant potato flakes	125 mL
1 cup	grated aged Cheddar cheese	250 mL
1/2 tsp	dry mustard	2 mL
1 1/4 tsp	bread machine yeast	6 mL

1. Measure ingredients into baking pan in the order recommended by the manufacturer. Insert pan into the oven chamber. Select **Basic Cycle**.

This rich, moist, black bread is a favorite of our 93-year-old, German-born neighbor, Christine Feenstra. With the sweetness of dates and apricots, it's perfect with fresh fruit and cheese for lunch.

Tip

If your machine does not have an "add ingredient" signal, add the dates and dried apricots after the flour.

Variation

Substitute chopped prunes or figs for the dates and dried apples for the apricots.

Christine's Fruited Pumpernickel

1.5 LB (750 G)

1 1/4 cups	water	300 mL
1 tbsp	vinegar	15 mL
1 1/4 tsp	salt	6 mL
1 tbsp	molasses	15 mL
1 tbsp	packed brown sugar	15 mL
2 tbsp	shortening	25 mL
2 3/4 cups	bread flour	675 mL
1/2 cup	rye flour	125 mL
1/3 cup	quartered dried apricots	75 mL
1/3 cup	whole pitted dates	75 mL
2 tsp	unsweetened cocoa	10 mL
2 tsp	instant coffee granules	10 mL
1/2 tsp	ground ginger	2 mL
1 3/4 tsp	bread machine yeast	8 mL

2 LB (1 KG)

1 1/2 cups	water	375 mL
2 tbsp	vinegar	25 mL
1 1/2 tsp	salt	7 mL
2 tbsp	molasses	25 mL
1 tbsp	packed brown sugar	15 mL
3 tbsp	shortening	45 mL
3 cups	bread flour	750 mL
3/4 cup	rye flour	175 mL
1/2 cup	quartered dried apricots	125 mL
1/2 cup	whole pitted dates	125 mL
1 tbsp	unsweetened cocoa	15 mL
1 tbsp	instant coffee granules	15 mL
1 tsp	ground ginger	5 mL
2 1/4 tsp	bread machine yeast	12 mL

1. Measure ingredients into baking pan in the order recommended by the manufacturer. Insert pan into the oven chamber. Select **Whole Wheat Cycle**.

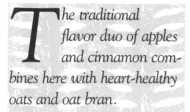

*T*he traditional
flavor duo of apples
and cinnamon com-
bines here with heart-healthy
oats and oat bran.

Tip

Use small- or medium-flaked, regular or quick-cooking oats, but not the "instant" variety.

Yes, you're reading it right: The 1.5 lb (750 g) recipe contains *more* yeast than the 2 lb (1 kg).

Variation

Substitute a grated or chopped small apple for the unsweetened applesauce.

Cinnamon Apple Oat

1.5 LB (750 G)

1/3 cup	water	75 mL
2/3 cup	unsweetened apple juice	150 mL
1/3 cup	unsweetened applesauce	75 mL
1 1/2 tsp	salt	7 mL
3 tbsp	honey	45 mL
2 tbsp	shortening	25 mL
3 cups	bread flour	750 mL
1/3 cup	quick-cooking oats	75 mL
1/4 cup	oat bran	50 mL
1 1/2 tsp	cinnamon	7 mL
2 1/4 tsp	bread machine yeast	12 mL

2 LB (1 KG)   L

1/2 cup	water	125 mL
3/4 cup	unsweetened apple juice	175 mL
1/2 cup	unsweetened applesauce	125 mL
1 1/2 tsp	salt	7 mL
1/4 cup	honey	50 mL
2 tbsp	shortening	25 mL
4 cups	bread flour	1000 mL
1/2 cup	quick-cooking oats	125 mL
1/3 cup	oat bran	75 mL
2 tsp	cinnamon	10 mL
1 1/4 tsp	bread machine yeast	6 mL

1. Measure ingredients into baking pan in the order recommended by the manufacturer. Insert pan into the oven chamber. Select **Basic Cycle.**

*E*njoy the texture of an English muffin, but not the work of cutting and grilling the small rounds? Just bake this loaf and toast each slice.

Tip

This recipe bakes an extra-large loaf — try the 1.5 lb (750 g) recipe first.

Yes, you're reading it right: The 1.5 lb (750 g) recipe contains *more* yeast than the 2 lb (1 kg).

Variation

Substitute 1 cup (250 mL) wheat-blend flour for an equal amount of white flour.

English Muffin Loaf

1.5 LB (750 G)

3/4 cup	milk (room temperature)	175 mL
2	eggs	2
1 tsp	salt	5 mL
2 tbsp	granulated sugar	25 mL
3 tbsp	shortening	45 mL
2 1/2 cups	bread flour	625 mL
1 3/4 tsp	bread machine yeast	8 mL

2 LB (1 KG)   L

1 cup	milk (room temperature)	250 mL
2	eggs	2
1 1/4 tsp	salt	6 mL
2 tbsp	granulated sugar	25 mL
3 tbsp	shortening	45 mL
3 cups	bread flour	750 mL
1 1/2 tsp	bread machine yeast	6 mL

1. Measure ingredients into baking pan in the order recommended by the manufacturer. Insert pan into the oven chamber. Select **Basic Cycle**.

*B*ritain's Hovis bread with a modern twist! Enjoy with Stilton cheese and red or black grapes.

Tip

Purchase malt syrup at a "brew your own" facility.

If your machine has a **Rapid Whole Wheat Cycle**, you can use it to bake either recipe; just increase the yeast by 3/4 tsp (4 mL).

Yes, you're reading it right: The 1.5 lb (750 g) recipe contains the *same* amount of yeast as the 2 lb (1 kg).

Variation

Add 1/3 to 1/2 cup (75 to 125 mL) raisins to increase sweetness naturally.

Malted Rye Bread

1.5 LB (750 G)

1 cup	water	250 mL
1/4 cup	nonfat dry milk	50 mL
1 1/4 tsp	salt	6 mL
1/4 cup	malt syrup	50 mL
2 tbsp	molasses	25 mL
2 tbsp	shortening	25 mL
1 1/2 cups	whole-wheat flour	375 mL
1 cup	bread flour	250 mL
1/2 cup	rye flour	125 mL
1 1/4 tsp	bread machine yeast	6 mL

2 LB (1 KG)

1 1/3 cups	water	325 mL
1/3 cup	nonfat dry milk	75 mL
1 1/2 tsp	salt	7 mL
1/4 cup	malt syrup	50 mL
3 tbsp	molasses	45 mL
2 tbsp	shortening	25 mL
1 3/4 cups	whole-wheat flour	425 mL
1 1/2 cups	bread flour	375 mL
1/2 cup	rye flour	125 mL
1 1/4 tsp	bread machine yeast	6 mL

1. Measure ingredients into baking pan in the order recommended by the manufacturer. Insert pan into the oven chamber. Select **Whole Wheat Cycle**.

*L*ooking for the per-
fect bread to serve
with a summer
salad? Look no further.
This one's a crowd pleaser!

Tip

No need to wait for the
sautéed mushrooms and
leeks to cool. Add immediately to the water in baking
pan.

Variation

According to sister Marilyn,
this is the best loaf to cube
or crumble for stuffing a
boneless pork loin roast.

Mushroom Leek

1.5 LB (750 G)

2 tbsp	butter	25 mL
1 1/2 cups	sliced mushrooms	375 mL
1/2 cup	sliced leeks	125 mL
1 tsp	dried thyme	5 mL
1 1/4 cups	water	300 mL
1 1/4 tsp	salt	6 mL
1 tbsp	honey	15 mL
1 cup	whole-wheat flour	250 mL
2 1/2 cups	bread flour	625 mL
3/4 tsp	bread machine yeast	4 mL

2 LB (1 KG)

2 tbsp	butter	25 mL
2 cups	sliced mushrooms	500 mL
3/4 cup	sliced leeks	175 mL
1 1/2 tsp	dried thyme	7 mL
1 1/3 cups	water	325 mL
1 1/2 tsp	salt	7 mL
2 tbsp	honey	25 mL
1 1/4 cups	whole-wheat flour	300 mL
3 1/4 cups	bread flour	800 mL
1 tsp	bread machine yeast	5 mL

1. In a saucepan heat butter over medium-high heat.
   Add mushrooms, leeks and thyme; sauté just until
   tender. Immediately place in baking pan. Measure
   remaining ingredients into baking pan in the order
   recommended by the manufacturer. Insert pan into
   the oven chamber. Select **Basic Cycle**.

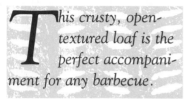

This crusty, open-textured loaf is the perfect accompaniment for any barbecue.

Tip

For an authentic, zesty flavor, use Reggiano Parmesan. It costs more, but it's worth it.

Pesto sauce is made from basil and pine nuts. It is sold in jars and is widely available in supermarkets.

Yes, you're reading it right: The 1.5 lb (750 g) recipe contains *more* yeast than the 2 lb (1 kg).

Variation

Add 1/3 to 1/2 cup (75 to 125 mL) pine nuts for an added crunch.

Use a combination of cheeses such as Parmesan and Emmental. Keep the total volume of cheese the same.

Pesto Loaf

1.5 LB (750 G)

1 1/4 cups	water	300 mL
1/4 cup	nonfat dry milk	50 mL
1 1/2 tsp	salt	7 mL
2 tbsp	granulated sugar	25 mL
2 tbsp	pesto sauce	25 mL
4 cups	bread flour	1000 mL
1/2 cup	grated Parmesan cheese	125 mL
1 1/2 tsp	bread machine yeast	8 mL

2 LB (1 KG)   L

1 1/2 cups	water	375 mL
1/3 cup	nonfat dry milk	75 mL
1 3/4 tsp	salt	8 mL
3 tbsp	granulated sugar	45 mL
3 tbsp	pesto sauce	45 mL
4 1/4 cups	bread flour	1050 mL
3/4 cup	grated Parmesan cheese	175 mL
1 1/2 tsp	bread machine yeast	7 mL

1. Measure ingredients into baking pan in the order recommended by the manufacturer. Insert pan into the oven chamber. Select **French Cycle** or **Basic Cycle**.

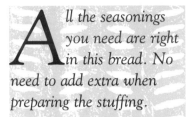

All the seasonings you need are right in this bread. No need to add extra when preparing the stuffing.

Tip

The 1.5 lb (750 g) loaf can be baked on a **Rapid One-Hour Basic Cycle**. The 2 lb (1 kg) loaf is too large to bake completely in this shorter length of time.

Yes, you're reading it right: The 1.5 lb (750 g) recipe contains the *same* amount of yeast as the 2 lb (1 kg).

Variation

To make croutons, cut the bread into 1-inch (2.5 cm) cubes, bake and toss with a bowl of crisp greens.

Quick Poultry-Stuffing Loaf

1 5 LB (750 G)

1 1/4 cups	water	300 mL
1/4 cup	nonfat dry milk	50 mL
1 1/4 tsp	salt	6 mL
2 tbsp	granulated sugar	25 mL
2 tbsp	shortening	25 mL
3 cups	bread flour	750 mL
2 tbsp	minced dried onion	25 mL
1 tbsp	dried parsley	15 mL
1 tbsp	dried rubbed sage	15 mL
1 tbsp	dried savory	15 mL
1 tsp	celery seeds	5 mL
1 tbsp	bread machine yeast	15 mL

2 LB (1 KG)

1 1/3 cups	water	325 mL
1/3 cup	nonfat dry milk	75 mL
1 1/2 tsp	salt	7 mL
3 tbsp	granulated sugar	45 mL
2 tbsp	shortening	25 mL
3 1/4 cups	bread flour	800 mL
3 tbsp	minced dried onion	45 mL
2 tbsp	dried parsley	25 mL
2 tbsp	dried rubbed sage	25 mL
2 tbsp	dried savory	25 mL
1 1/2 tsp	celery seeds	7 mL
1 tbsp	bread machine yeast	15 mL

1. Measure ingredients into baking pan in the order recommended by the manufacturer. Insert pan into the oven chamber. Select **Rapid Two-Hour Basic Cycle**.

*C*harles Pearson, a Bread Basket subscriber in Kingston, tells us that this aromatic, heavy-textured loaf has been a hit with his family for years.

Tip

Use triple the amount of fresh herbs for dried. Wash and dry well before snipping with kitchen shears.

Yes, you're reading it right: The 1.5 lb (750 g) recipe contains *more* yeast than the 2 lb (1 kg).

Variation

Substitute different herbs — try summer savory, red basil and a variegated thyme.

San Francisco Firehouse Bread

1.5 LB (750 G)

1 cup	evaporated milk	250 mL
1/2 cup	water	125 mL
1 1/4 tsp	salt	6 mL
3 tbsp	granulated sugar	45 mL
2 tbsp	vegetable oil	25 mL
1 3/4 cups	whole-wheat flour	425 mL
1 1/2 cups	bread flour	375 mL
1/3 cup	cornmeal	75 mL
2 tbsp	minced dried onion	25 mL
1 tbsp	dried parsley	15 mL
1 1/4 tsp	dried rubbed sage	6 mL
1 tsp	dried dill	5 mL
1 3/4 tsp	bread machine yeast	8 mL

2 LB (1 KG)

1	can (13 oz [385 mL]) evaporated milk	1
3/4 cup	water	175 mL
1 1/2 tsp	salt	7 mL
1/4 cup	granulated sugar	50 mL
3 tbsp	vegetable oil	45 mL
2 1/4 cups	whole-wheat flour	550 mL
1 1/2 cups	bread flour	375 mL
1/2 cup	cornmeal	125 mL
3 tbsp	minced dried onion	45 mL
1 tbsp	dried parsley	15 mL
1 3/4 tsp	dried rubbed sage	8 mL
1 1/4 tsp	dried dill	6 mL
1 tsp	bread machine yeast	5 mL

1. Measure ingredients into baking pan in the order recommended by the manufacturer. Insert pan into the oven chamber. Select **Whole Wheat Cycle**.

HEALTHY AND HEARTY GRAINS

BAKING WITH GRAINS	28
CUMIN RYE BREAD	29
DOUBLE-CRUNCH WHEAT BREAD	30
GRANARY BREAD	31
GRANOLA CURRANT LOAF	32
MOCK SPOON BREAD	33
OLD-FASHIONED WHEAT BREAD	34
ONION RYE LOAF	35
RAISIN BRAN LOAF	36
SESAME SEMOLINA BREAD	37
TRIPLE-WHEAT BREAD	38
WILD RICE AND CRANBERRY LOAF	39
YOGURT WHEAT-GERM BREAD	40

Today's health-conscious consumers are including more and more grains in their meals and snacks. These breads are a grain-lovers delight.

BAKING WITH GRAINS

• Purchase grains in small quantities and refrigerate to prevent the fat (contained in the germ of the grain kernel) from turning rancid. If stored longer than 1 month, taste before using.

• Do not use instant oats in recipes that call for rolled oats; the bread texture will be too wet and compact. Medium-or large-flake, regular or quick-cooking oats produce the best loaf.

• Cracked wheat, bulgur and other grains absorb the water and the resulting loaf can be short, heavy and compact in texture. This is especially important when using the timer. To prevent grains from touching the water, level the flour into the corners of the baking pan, then measure grains on top.

• An equal amount of bulgur can be substituted for cracked wheat.

• Bran has the effect of cutting the gluten strands, thus weakening their ability to trap air. Don't increase the amount of bran stated in the recipe or the loaf could collapse.

• The recipes in this book have been developed for unsweetened (not sweetened) cereals. If only sweetened Muesli or granola are available, decrease the sugar in the recipe.

• For a contrast in texture and appearance, sprinkle extra oatmeal or barley flakes on top of the risen dough just before baking in a conventional oven or before the baking cycle of bread machine begins. Open and close the lid quickly so no heat escapes.

*I*f you enjoy a lighter-textured rye, then this is the bread for you!

Tip

For more fiber and nutrients, replace 1 cup (250 mL) of the bread flour with whole-wheat flour.

Variation

Substitute malt syrup for the corn syrup.

Try caraway and fennel seeds instead of the cumin and anise seeds.

Cumin Rye Bread

1.5 LB (750 G)

1 1/4 cups	water	300 mL
1/4 cup	nonfat dry milk	50 mL
1 1/4 tsp	salt	6 mL
2 tbsp	corn syrup	25 mL
2 tbsp	shortening	25 mL
3 cups	bread flour	750 mL
3/4 cup	rye flour	175 mL
2 tsp	cumin seeds	10 mL
2 tsp	anise seeds	10 mL
1 tsp	bread machine yeast	5 mL

2 LB (1 KG)

1 1/2 cups	water	375 mL
1/3 cup	nonfat dry milk	75 mL
1 1/2 tsp	salt	7 mL
3 tbsp	corn syrup	45 mL
2 tbsp	shortening	25 mL
3 1/2 cups	bread flour	875 mL
1 cup	rye flour	250 mL
1 tbsp	cumin seeds	15 mL
2 tsp	anise seeds	10 mL
1 1/4 tsp	bread machine yeast	6 mL

1. Measure all ingredients into baking pan in the order recommended by the manufacturer. Insert pan into the oven chamber. Select **Basic Cycle**.

*F*rench toast made from this bread is scrumptious — the perfect treat for a holiday brunch.

Tip

Don't use roasted salted sunflower seeds for this recipe. The fat and salt will make the loaf short and heavy.

Variation

For an even crunchier loaf, substitute bulgur for the cracked wheat.

Double-Crunch Wheat Bread

1.5 LB (750 G)

1 1/3 cups	water	325 mL
1/4 cup	nonfat dry milk	50 mL
1 tsp	salt	5 mL
2 tbsp	honey	25 mL
2 tbsp	vegetable oil	25 mL
3 cups	bread flour	750 mL
2/3 cup	cracked wheat	150 mL
2/3 cup	raw unsalted sunflower seeds	150 mL
1 tsp	bread machine yeast	5 mL

2 LB (1 KG)

1 1/2 cups	water	375 mL
1/3 cup	nonfat dry milk	75 mL
1 1/4 tsp	salt	6 mL
3 tbsp	honey	45 mL
2 tbsp	vegetable oil	25 mL
3 1/4 cups	bread flour	800 mL
3/4 cup	cracked wheat	175 mL
3/4 cup	raw unsalted sunflower seeds	175 mL
1 1/4 tsp	bread machine yeast	6 mL

1. Measure ingredients into baking pan in the order recommended by the manufacturer. Insert pan into the oven chamber. Select **Basic Cycle**.

*Y*ou won't find many breads with such a collection of grains — wheat, buckwheat, oats, barley and rye. The name says it all!

Tip

Remember that only wheat and rye contain gluten. Increasing the amount of other grains will result in an even heavier loaf.

See the Techniques Glossary (page 183) for instructions on cooking rye groats.

Yes, you're reading it right: The 1.5 lb (750 g) recipe contains *more* yeast than the 2 lb (1 kg).

Variation

Substitute quinoa, spelt, amaranth or kamut for one or more of the grains, but not the bread flour.

Granary Bread

1.5 LB (750 G)

1 1/4 cups	water	300 mL
1/4 cup	nonfat dry milk	50 mL
1 1/2 tsp	salt	7 mL
2 tbsp	packed brown sugar	25 mL
1 tbsp	molasses	15 mL
2 tbsp	shortening	25 mL
2 3/4 cups	bread flour	675 mL
1/4 cup	buckwheat flour	50 mL
1/4 cup	quick-cooking oats	50 mL
1/4 cup	barley flakes	50 mL
1/4 cup	cooked rye groats	50 mL
1 1/4 tsp	bread machine yeast	6 mL

2 LB (1 KG)

1 1/2 cups	water	375 mL
1/3 cup	nonfat dry milk	75 mL
1 3/4 tsp	salt	8 mL
2 tbsp	packed brown sugar	25 mL
2 tbsp	molasses	25 mL
2 tbsp	shortening	25 mL
3 1/2 cups	bread flour	875 mL
1/3 cup	buckwheat flour	75 mL
1/3 cup	quick-cooking oats	75 mL
1/3 cup	barley flakes	75 mL
1/3 cup	cooked rye groats	75 mL
1 tsp	bread machine yeast	5 mL

1. Measure ingredients into baking pan in the order recommended by the manufacturer. Insert pan into the oven chamber. Select **Whole Wheat Cycle**.

ried currants are a traditional staple of holiday baking. This bread is sure to bring back fond memories.

Tip

Unsweetened granola can be purchased at bulk food stores. If all you can find is the sweetened variety, decrease the sugar by half.

Yes, you're reading it right: The 1.5 lb (750 g) recipe contains *more* yeast than the 2 lb (1 kg).

Variation

For a nuttier, slightly sweeter taste, substitute an equal amount of Muesli for the granola and raisins for the dried currants.

Granola Currant Loaf

1.5 LB (750 G)

1 1/4 cups	water	300 mL
1/4 cup	nonfat dry milk	50 mL
1 1/2 tsp	salt	7 mL
2 tbsp	packed brown sugar	25 mL
1 tbsp	vegetable oil	15 mL
2 3/4 cups	bread flour	675 mL
1 cup	granola	250 mL
1 1/2 tsp	bread machine yeast	7 mL
1/2 cup	dried currants	125 mL

2 LB (1 KG)

1 1/2 cups	water	375 mL
1/3 cup	nonfat dry milk	75 mL
1 3/4 tsp	salt	8 mL
2 tbsp	packed brown sugar	25 mL
2 tbsp	vegetable oil	25 mL
3 1/4 cups	bread flour	800 mL
1 1/4 cups	granola	300 mL
1 1/4 tsp	bread machine yeast	6 mL
3/4 cup	dried currants	175 mL

1. Measure all ingredients *except dried currants* into baking pan in the order recommended by the manufacturer. Insert pan into the oven chamber. Select **Basic Cycle**. Add currants at the "add ingredient" signal.

ASIAGO HERB LOAF (PAGE 14) ➤

If you love cornbread, the sharp Cheddar and smoky bacon flavors in this bread will make you think you've gone to heaven.

Tip

For cheese weight/volume equivalents, see Ingredient Glossary (page 177).

Yes, you're reading it right: The 1.5 lb (750 g) recipe contains the *same* amount of yeast as the 2 lb (1 kg).

Variation

Substitute 3 to 4 oz (90 to 120 g) of cooked smoked ham for the bacon.

Mock Spoon Bread

1.5 LB (750 G)

1/4 cup	milk	50 mL
1	can (10 oz [284 mL]) cream-style corn	1
1 tsp	salt	5 mL
1 tbsp	honey	15 mL
2 3/4 cups	bread flour	675 mL
3	slices crisp bacon, crumbled	3
1/3 cup	cornmeal	75 mL
1/2 cup	grated aged Cheddar cheese	125 mL
1 1/4 tsp	bread machine yeast	6 mL

2 LB (1 KG)

1/2 cup	milk	125 mL
1	can (10 oz [284 mL]) cream-style corn	1
1 tsp	salt	5 mL
1 tbsp	honey	15 mL
3 cups	bread flour	750 mL
4	slices crisp bacon, crumbled	4
1/2 cup	cornmeal	125 mL
3/4 cup	grated aged Cheddar cheese	175 mL
1 tsp	bread machine yeast	5 mL

1. Measure ingredients into baking pan in the order recommended by the manufacturer. Insert pan into the oven chamber. Select **Basic Cycle**.

≺ WILD RICE AND CRANBERRY LOAF (PAGE 39)

*I*f you find that most 100% whole wheat breads are too heavy, try this one. It's lighter in texture than the traditional loaf.

Tip

If your machine has a **Rapid Whole Wheat Cycle**, you can bake either size recipe; double the yeast for the 2 lb (1 kg) and increase the 1.5 lb (750 g) by 1/2 tsp (2 mL).

Yes, you're reading it right: The 1.5 lb (750 g) recipe contains *more* yeast than the 2 lb (1 kg).

Variation

For a sweeter, milder-flavored bread, substitute packed brown sugar for the honey and the molasses.

Old-Fashioned Wheat Bread

1.5 LB (750 G)

1 1/2 cups	water	375 mL
1/4 cup	nonfat dry milk	50 mL
1 1/2 tsp	salt	7 mL
2 tbsp	honey	25 mL
1 tbsp	molasses	15 mL
2 tbsp	vegetable oil	25 mL
2 1/2 cups	whole-wheat flour	625 mL
1 cup	bread flour	250 mL
1/4 cup	gluten	50 mL
1 1/4 tsp	bread machine yeast	6 mL

2 LB (1 KG)

1 3/4 cups	water	425 mL
1/3 cup	nonfat dry milk	75 mL
1 1/2 tsp	salt	7 mL
2 tbsp	honey	25 mL
2 tbsp	molasses	25 mL
2 tbsp	vegetable oil	25 mL
2 3/4 cups	whole-wheat flour	675 mL
1 1/4 cups	bread flour	300 mL
1/4 cup	gluten	50 mL
3/4 tsp	bread machine yeast	4 mL

1. Measure ingredients into baking pan in the order recommended by the manufacturer. Insert pan into the oven chamber. Select **Whole Wheat Cycle**.

*T*he mellow onion flavor of this robust rye makes for outstanding cold roast beef sandwiches. Just add a little Dijon mustard.

Tip

Do not substitute fresh onion for the dried flakes — moisture content is too high, and you'll end up with a short, weak-flavored loaf.

The 1.5 lb (750 g) loaf is perfect for a small slice.

Variation

Replace 1 cup (250 mL) of the bread flour with 1 cup (250 mL) whole-wheat flour.

Onion Rye Loaf

1.5 LB (750 G)

1 1/4 cups	water	300 mL
1/4 cup	nonfat dry milk	50 mL
1 tsp	salt	5 mL
2 tbsp	packed brown sugar	25 mL
2 tbsp	shortening	25 mL
2 1/2 cups	bread flour	650 mL
1/2 cup	rye flour	125 mL
1/4 cup	dried onion flakes	50 mL
1 1/4 tsp	bread machine yeast	5 mL

2 LB (1 KG)

1 1/2 cups	water	375 mL
1/3 cup	nonfat dry milk	75 mL
1 1/2 tsp	salt	7 mL
3 tbsp	packed brown sugar	45 mL
3 tbsp	shortening	45 mL
3 2/3 cups	bread flour	900 mL
2/3 cup	rye flour	150 mL
1/3 cup	dried onion flakes	75 mL
1 1/2 tsp	bread machine yeast	7 mL

1. Measure ingredients into baking pan in the order recommended by the manufacturer. Insert pan into the oven chamber. Select **Basic Cycle**.

*E*njoy bran muffins for breakfast? Toast a thick slice of this loaf for a rich molasses treat.

Tip

The higher the bran content of the cereal, the closer this is to a real bran muffin.

Variation

Substitute oat bran for the wheat bran and dates or other dried fruit for the raisins.

Raisin Bran Loaf

1.5 LB (750 G)

1 1/4 cups	water	300 mL
1/4 cup	nonfat dry milk	50 mL
1 1/2 tsp	salt	7 mL
2 tbsp	packed brown sugar	25 mL
1 tbsp	molasses	15 mL
2 tbsp	vegetable oil	25 mL
1 cup	whole-wheat flour	250 mL
1 1/2 cups	bread flour	375 mL
1/2 cup	bran cereal	125 mL
1/4 cup	wheat bran	50 mL
3/4 cup	raisins	175 mL
1 1/4 tsp	bread machine yeast	6 mL

2 LB (1 KG)

1 1/2 cups	water	375 mL
1/3 cup	nonfat dry milk	75 mL
1 3/4 tsp	salt	8 mL
3 tbsp	packed brown sugar	45 mL
2 tbsp	molasses	25 mL
2 tbsp	vegetable oil	25 mL
1 1/4 cups	whole-wheat flour	300 mL
1 3/4 cups	bread flour	425 mL
3/4 cup	bran cereal	175 mL
1/2 cup	wheat bran	125 mL
1 cup	raisins	250 mL
1 1/2 tsp	bread machine yeast	7 mL

1. Measure ingredients into baking pan in the order recommended by the manufacturer. Insert pan into the oven chamber. Select **Whole Wheat Cycle**.

*R*eminiscent of a cornbread, but finer textured, this loaf makes a nice contrast in a a basket of darker grain breads.

Tip

Look for semolina flour in bulk food stores or in the pasta or specialty food section of your supermarket.

Yes, you're reading it right: The 1.5 lb (750 g) recipe contains the *same* amount of yeast as the 2 lb (1 kg).

Variation

Pasta flour or a very fine grind cornmeal can be substituted for the semolina.

Sesame Semolina Bread

1.5 LB (750 G)

1 1/4 cups	water	300 mL
1/4 cup	nonfat dry milk	50 mL
1 1/4 tsp	salt	6 mL
2 tbsp	granulated sugar	25 mL
2 tbsp	olive oil	25 mL
2 1/4 cups	bread flour	550 mL
1 cup	semolina flour	250 mL
1/3 cup	sesame seeds	75 mL
1 1/4 tsp	bread machine yeast	6 mL

2 LB (1 KG)

1 1/2 cups	water	375 mL
1/3 cup	nonfat dry milk	75 mL
1 1/2 tsp	salt	7 mL
2 tbsp	granulated sugar	25 mL
3 tbsp	olive oil	45 mL
2 3/4 cups	bread flour	675 mL
1 cup	semolina flour	250 mL
1/2 cup	sesame seeds	125 mL
1 1/4 tsp	bread machine yeast	6 mL

1. Measure ingredients into baking pan in the order recommended by the manufacturer. Insert pan into the oven chamber. Select **Basic Cycle**.

*T*his loaf is shorter than some, but with its great flavor and high fiber content, you're sure not to mind.

Tip

See the Techniques Glossary (page 183) for instructions on cooking wheat berries.

Variation

Substitute any wheat-blend flour for the total amount of whole-wheat flour and flaxseeds.

Triple-Wheat Bread

1.5 LB (750 G)

1 1/3 cups	water	325 mL
1/4 cup	nonfat dry milk	50 mL
1 1/2 tsp	salt	7 mL
3 tbsp	honey	45 mL
2 tbsp	vegetable oil	25 mL
1 1/4 cups	whole-wheat flour	300 mL
2 cups	bread flour	500 mL
1/3 cup	cooked wheat berries	75 mL
1/3 cup	cracked wheat	75 mL
1/3 cup	flaxseeds	75 mL
1 1/4 tsp	bread machine yeast	6 mL

2 LB (1 KG)

1 1/2 cups	water	375 mL
1/3 cup	nonfat dry milk	75 mL
1 3/4 tsp	salt	8 mL
1/4 cup	honey	50 mL
3 tbsp	vegetable oil	45 mL
1 1/4 cups	whole-wheat flour	300 mL
2 cups	bread flour	500 mL
1/2 cup	cooked wheat berries	125 mL
1/2 cup	cracked wheat	125 mL
1/2 cup	flaxseeds	125 mL
1 1/2 tsp	bread machine yeast	7 mL

1. Measure ingredients into baking pan in the order recommended by the manufacturer. Insert pan into the oven chamber. Select **Whole Wheat Cycle**.

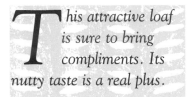

This attractive loaf is sure to bring compliments. Its nutty taste is a real plus.

Tip

Prepare extra wild rice when cooking your favorite duck or goose dinner. Store in the refrigerator until needed.

See Techniques Glossary (page 183) for instructions on cooking wild rice.

Yes, you're reading it right: The 1.5 lb (750 g) recipe contains the *same* amount of yeast as the 2 lb (1 kg).

Variation

Substitute raw, unsalted sunflower seeds or unsalted peanuts for the pine nuts and dried blueberries or dried sour cherries for the dried cranberries.

Wild Rice and Cranberry Loaf

1.5 LB (750 G)

1 1/4 cups	water	300 mL
1/4 cup	nonfat dry milk	50 mL
1 1/4 tsp	salt	6 mL
2 tbsp	honey	25 mL
1 tbsp	olive oil	15 mL
3 1/3 cups	bread flour	825 mL
3/4 cup	cooked wild rice	175 mL
1/4 cup	pine nuts	50 mL
3/4 tsp	celery seeds	4 mL
1/8 tsp	black pepper	0.5 mL
1 tsp	bread machine yeast	5 mL
2/3 cup	dried cranberries	150 mL

2 LB (1 KG)

1 1/2 cups	water	375 mL
1/3 cup	nonfat dry milk	75 mL
1 1/2 tsp	salt	7 mL
2 tbsp	honey	25 mL
1 tbsp	olive oil	15 mL
4 cups	bread flour	1000 mL
1 cup	cooked wild rice	250 mL
1/3 cup	pine nuts	75 mL
1 tsp	celery seeds	5 mL
1/8 tsp	black pepper	0.5 mL
1 tsp	bread machine yeast	5 mL
3/4 cup	dried cranberries	175 mL

1. Measure all ingredients *except dried cranberries* into baking pan in the order recommended by the manufacturer. Insert pan into the oven chamber. Select **Basic Cycle**. Add dried cranberries at the "add ingredient" signal.

Looking for a super-healthy bread with lots of fiber? Try this open-textured, nutritious loaf!

Tip

Wheat germ is one of the best sources of vitamin E. Purchase small quantities and store in the refrigerator.

Yes, you're reading it right: The 1.5 lb (750 g) recipe contains *more* yeast than the 2 lb (1 kg).

Variation

Reduce the amount of fat in this recipe by using no-fat or low-fat yogurt.

Yogurt Wheat-Germ Bread

1.5 LB (750 G)

2/3 cup	water	150 mL
2/3 cup	plain yogurt	150 mL
1 1/2 tsp	salt	7 mL
2 tbsp	honey	25 mL
1 tbsp	vegetable oil	15 mL
1/2 cup	whole-wheat flour	125 mL
2 1/4 cups	bread flour	550 mL
2 tbsp	wheat bran	25 mL
2 tbsp	wheat germ	25 mL
1 1/2 tsp	bread machine yeast	8 mL

2 LB (1 KG)

1 cup	water	250 mL
3/4 cup	plain yogurt	175 mL
1 3/4 tsp	salt	8 mL
3 tbsp	honey	45 mL
2 tbsp	vegetable oil	25 mL
1 cup	whole-wheat flour	250 mL
3 cups	bread flour	750 mL
3 tbsp	wheat bran	45 mL
3 tbsp	wheat germ	45 mL
1 1/4 tsp	bread machine yeast	6 mL

1. Measure ingredients into baking pan in the order recommended by the manufacturer. Insert pan into the oven chamber. Select **Basic Cycle**.

FLAVORFUL FILLED AND FLATBREADS

TIPS FOR PREPARING FILLINGS   42

SPINACH PITAS   43

NEW ORLEANS-STYLE MUFFALETTA   44

RED ONION FOCACCIA   46

MOROCCAN ANISE BREAD   47

ROASTED VEGETABLE-STUFFED CALZONES   48

SAUSAGE-STUFFED STROMBOLI   50

SUN-DRIED TOMATO LAVOSH   52

TURKEY-FILLED CHEESE BRAID   54

TOMATO ROSEMARY CIABATTA   56

Prepare these breads for a luncheon treat or when company calls.
Add a crisp salad and the menu is complete.

TIPS FOR PREPARING FILLINGS

• Vegetables for fillings should be cut into pieces large enough to be seen and recognized, but not so large that the filled bread falls apart when eaten.

• Ground-meat fillings must be completely cooked before enclosing in the dough since they do not cook as the bread bakes.

• In order to minimize the fat in fillings, and to prevent soggy bread crusts, always sauté vegetables or brown meats using a minimum of oil. Drain well before enclosing in dough.

• Quickly cool all fillings to room temperature before enclosing in dough. If the filling is too hot, it may kill the yeast, and the dough immediately surrounding the filling may be gummy.

• Spread the filling right to the ends of the dough so that the first and last slices have the same amount of filling as those in the middle.

• Cool meat- or cheese-filled breads quickly and refrigerate following baking. Refrigerate leftovers. Serve warm or cold.

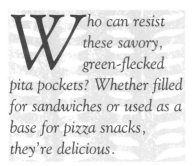

*W*ho can resist these savory, green-flecked pita pockets? Whether filled for sandwiches or used as a base for pizza snacks, they're delicious.

Tip

Don't make the pitas too thick or a pocket won't form.

Be sure to squeeze the moisture out of the spinach before measuring.

Variation

Enjoy warm pitas packed with exotic grains and roasted vegetables.

Divide dough into smaller portions for mini-pitas (children love them) or use for hors d'ouevres.

Spinach Pitas

Makes 20 pitas

Baking sheet *or* baking stone or baking tile, unglazed

1 1/4 cups	water	300 mL
1/4 cup	chopped thawed frozen spinach	50 mL
1	egg	1
1 1/2 tsp	salt	7 mL
2 tsp	granulated sugar	10 mL
2 tbsp	shortening	25 mL
1 cup	whole-wheat flour	250 mL
3 cups	bread flour	750 mL
1/2 cup	buttermilk powder	125 mL
1 1/2 tsp	bread machine yeast	7 mL

1. Measure ingredients into machine's baking pan in the order recommended by the manufacturer. Insert pan into the oven chamber. Select **Dough Cycle**.

2. Remove dough to a lightly floured surface. Cover with a large bowl and let rest for 10 to 15 minutes. Divide the dough into 20 portions. Form each into a ball and then flatten with your fingertips, working in as much flour as possible. Roll out into 4- to 5-inch (10 to 12.5 cm) circles, 1/8 inch (2 mm) thick. Meanwhile, preheat oven to 450° F (230° C).

3. Place oven rack in bottom third of the oven. If using baking stone or baking tile, preheat in oven for 15 minutes. Place 3 to 4 pitas on baking sheet or heated baking stone or tile. Bake in preheated oven for 3 to 4 minutes. For soft pitas, do not allow to brown. Immediately upon removing from the oven, stack the puffed pitas. Wrap in a towel while cooling.

Here's our version of a Tex-Mex muffaletta, stuffed with chicken and Monterey Jack, and seasoned with a balsamic-and-herb vinaigrette.

Tip

Refrigerating the stuffed muffaletta before baking allows the flavors to blend and the interior of the bread to soften.

Variation

Use leftover bread from the muffaletta to make croutons or bread crumbs.

New Orleans-Style Muffaletta

Makes 1 muffaletta, serving 8

Baking sheet, lightly greased

Bread

1 1/4 cups	water	300 mL
1 1/2 tsp	salt	7 mL
2 tbsp	packed brown sugar	25 mL
2 tbsp	olive oil	25 mL
1 1/2 cups	whole-wheat flour	375 mL
1 1/2 cups	bread flour	375 mL
3/4 cup	7-grain cereal	175 mL
1/2 cup	buttermilk powder	125 mL
1 1/4 tsp	bread machine yeast	6 mL

Muffaletta Filling

1	red bell pepper, seeded and diced	1
1	yellow pepper, seeded and diced	1
1	large tomato, diced	1
2	cloves garlic, minced	2
1/4 cup	store-bought balsamic-and-herb vinaigrette	50 mL
12 oz	lean chicken breast, thinly sliced	375 g
6 oz	Monterey Jack cheese, grated	175 g

1. Measure the bread ingredients into machine's baking pan in the order recommended by the manufacturer. Insert pan into the oven chamber. Select **Dough Cycle**.

2. Filling: In a large glass bowl, combine red pepper, yellow pepper, tomato and garlic. Add vinaigrette and toss to coat. Marinate for at least 2 hours in the refrigerator.

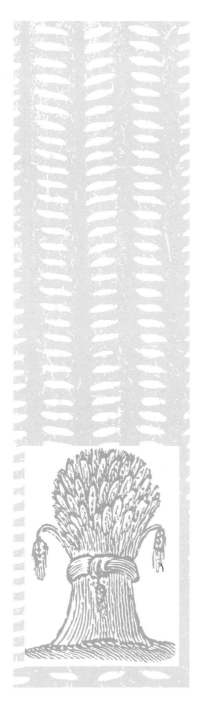

3. Remove dough to a lightly floured surface. Cover with a large bowl and let rest for 10 to 15 minutes. Form into one 5-inch (12.5 cm) round loaf with a high-rounded top. Place on prepared baking sheet. Cover and let rise in a warm, draft-free place for 30 to 45 minutes or until doubled in volume. Meanwhile, preheat oven to 350° F (180° C).

4. Transfer dough to preheated oven and bake for 40 to 50 minutes or until loaf sounds hollow when tapped on the bottom. Set aside to cool completely. Using a serrated knife, cut 1 inch (2.5 cm) off the top of the bread; set the top aside. Cut out center of loaf, leaving at least 1/2 inch (1 cm) of bread on bottom and sides. Cut out top, leaving 1/4 inch (5 mm) of bread.

5. Spread one-third of the pepper mixture on bottom of muffaletta. Top with one-half chicken and then one-half cheese. Repeat with one more layer of pepper mixture, chicken and cheese. Add remaining pepper mixture. Replace reserved bread top. Wrap tightly in plastic wrap, twisting ends to secure, and refrigerate for at least 8 hours. Cut into 8 wedges.

*E*veryone's favorite for take-out lunches, this focaccia is easily prepared in your bread machine.

Tip

Put a few slices of deli meats and cheese into a split focaccia and grill until warmed through. Add roasted yellow peppers, sliced tomatoes and alfalfa sprouts.

For instructions on sweating vegetables, see Techniques Glossary (page 183).

Variation

Form the dough into two 9- to 10-inch (23 to 25 cm) round focaccia, about 1 inch (2.5 cm) thick. Brush with olive oil and dried herbs or add your favorite topping before baking.

Red Onion Focaccia

Makes 2 focaccia

Two 8-inch (2 L) round baking pans, lightly greased

1 tbsp	olive oil	15 mL
1 cup	chopped red onions	250 mL
2	cloves garlic, crushed	2
1 1/3 cups	water	325 mL
1 1/2 tsp	salt	7 mL
1 tsp	granulated sugar	5 mL
1 tbsp	olive oil	15 mL
4 1/4 cups	bread flour	1050 mL
1 1/2 tsp	bread machine yeast	7 mL

1. In a frying pan, heat oil over medium heat. Add red onions and garlic; cook until tender but not browned. Place in machine's baking pan. Measure remaining ingredients into baking pan in the order recommended by the manufacturer. Insert pan into the oven chamber. Select **Dough Cycle**.

2. Remove dough to a lightly floured surface. Cover with a large bowl and let rest for 10 to 15 minutes. Divide the dough in half. Stretch each into prepared pans. Dimple with flour-coated fingers. Cover and let rise in a warm, draft-free place for 30 minutes or until not quite doubled in volume. Meanwhile, preheat oven to 400° F (200° C).

3. Re-dimple dough and bake in preheated oven on lowest rack for 20 to 30 minutes or until focaccia sounds hollow when tapped on the bottom.

M*aking dough doesn't get much easier (or faster) than this. Hands-on preparation time is less than 15 minutes.*

Tip

Baking the flatbread directly on the oven rack gives a crispier bottom crust.

Variation

Roll out the dough to one 10-inch (25 cm) circle and finish as a hearth bread.

Moroccan Anise Bread

Makes 2

Baking sheet, sprinkled with cornmeal

1 1/3 cups	water	325 mL
1 1/2 tsp	salt	7 mL
1 1/2 cups	whole-wheat flour	375 mL
2 cups	bread flour	500 mL
1/4 cup	cornmeal	50 mL
2 tsp	anise seeds	10 mL
1 tsp	bread machine yeast	5 mL

1. Measure ingredients into machine's baking pan in the order recommended by the manufacturer. Insert pan into the oven chamber. Select **Dough Cycle**.

2. Remove dough to a lightly floured surface. Cover with a large bowl and let rest for 10 to 15 minutes. Divide dough in half. Form or roll out each half into a 10-inch (25 cm) round. Place on prepared baking sheet. Cover and let rise in a warm, draft-free place for 20 to 25 minutes or until almost doubled in volume. Meanwhile, preheat oven to 400° F (200° C).

3. Pierce the dough all the way through with a fork. Bake in preheated oven for 10 minutes. Remove from baking sheet and place directly onto the oven rack; continue baking for 8 to 10 minutes or until flatbreads sound hollow when tapped on the bottom.

These stuffed mini-pizzas are great for lunch or snacks.

Tip

To prevent a soggy crust, be sure to drain the filling well before enclosing in dough.

Variation

For a totally different shape, try making Roasted Vegetable Cups. See page 184 for instructions.

Roasted Vegetable-Stuffed Calzones

Makes 12

Roasting pan
Baking sheet, lightly greased

Bread

1 1/3 cups	water	325 mL
1 1/4 tsp	salt	6 mL
2 tbsp	granulated sugar	25 mL
2 tbsp	shortening	25 mL
3 2/3 cups	bread flour	900 mL
1 tsp	bread machine yeast	5 mL

Roasted Vegetable Filling

1	small Italian eggplant, cut into 1-inch (2.5 cm) pieces	1
1	large onion, cut into 1-inch (2.5 cm) pieces	1
1	large red bell pepper, cut into 1-inch (2.5 cm) pieces	1
1	large yellow pepper, cut into 1-inch (2.5 cm) pieces	1
1	medium zucchini, cut into 1-inch (2.5 cm) pieces	1
1 tbsp	roasted-garlic-and-basil-flavored olive oil	15 mL
6	cloves garlic, minced	6
1 tbsp	dried oregano	15 mL

1. Measure the bread ingredients into machine's baking pan in the order recommended by the manufacturer. Insert pan into the oven chamber. Select **Dough Cycle**.

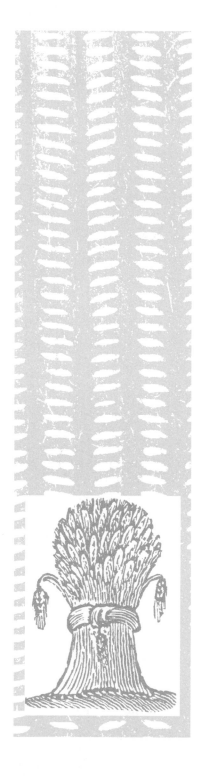

2. Filling: Add eggplant to roasting pan, along with onion, red pepper, yellow pepper and zucchini. Brush with oil and sprinkle with garlic and oregano. Roast vegetables in preheated oven, turning once during cooking, for 20 to 30 minutes or until tender. Do not overcook. Set aside to cool.

3. Remove dough to a lightly floured surface. Cover with a large bowl and let rest for 10 to 15 minutes. Divide the dough into 12 portions. Roll out each into a 5-inch (12.5 cm) circle. Place an equal amount of filling on one-half of each circle. Fold unfilled half over the filled half, sealing the edges tightly. Place on prepared baking sheet. Cover and let rise in a warm, draft-free place for 30 to 45 minutes or until doubled in volume. Meanwhile, preheat oven to 375° F (190° C).

4. Bake in preheated oven for 25 to 35 minutes or until calzones sound hollow when tapped on the bottom.

*S*tromboli, a specialty of Philadelphia, is a calzone-like sandwich of meat and cheese, usually pepperoni and mozzarella.

Tip

Prepare ahead for any occasion or quick meal. Tightly wrap the unrisen dough and freeze for up to 4 weeks. Thaw in the refrigerator for 6 to 8 hours. Let rise 20 to 45 minutes in a warm, draft-free place then bake as directed in recipe.

Sausage-Stuffed Stromboli

Makes 1 stromboli

Baking sheet, lightly greased

Bread

1 1/2 cups	water	375 mL
1 1/2 tsp	salt	7 mL
2 tbsp	granulated sugar	25 mL
4 cups	bread flour	1000 mL
1 1/4 tsp	bread machine yeast	6 mL

Sausage Filling

1 lb	pork sausage, casings removed, meat crumbled	500 g
3	medium carrots, chopped	3
3	medium leeks, chopped	3
1 tbsp	dry rubbed rosemary	15 mL
3/4 cup	sliced mushrooms	175 mL
2 tbsp	dry white wine	25 mL

Glaze

1	egg yolk	1
1 tbsp	water	15 mL

1. Measure the bread ingredients into machine's baking pan in the order suggested by the manufacturer. Insert baking pan into the oven chamber. Select **Dough Cycle**.

2. Filling: In a large frying pan, brown sausage meat; drain well and set aside. In same frying pan, sauté carrots, leeks and mushrooms. Add browned sausage meat and white wine. Mix gently and set aside to cool.

3. Remove dough to a lightly floured surface. Cover with a large bowl and let rest for 10 to 15 minutes. Roll out dough to a 16- by 13-inch (40 by 32.5 cm) rectangle. Place on prepared baking sheet. Cut 2-inch (5 cm) squares out of each corner. Spread cooled filling down the center 6 inches (15 cm), omitting narrow ends.

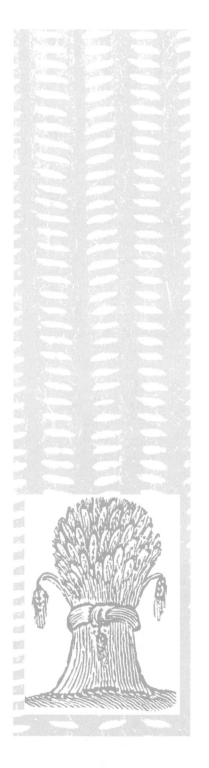

4. Glaze: In a small bowl, whisk together egg yolk and water until smooth. Brush the glaze around the cut corners. Fold short ends of dough over filling. Brush with glaze. With scissors, make cuts on the long side, 1 inch (2.5 cm) apart, from edge of the dough to within 3/4 inch (2 cm) of the filling. Repeat on remaining side. Fold alternately, into the center, crisscrossing strips over the filling, at the same time stretching a little to bring the uncut dough up and over the filling. Cover and let rise in a warm, draft-free place for 20 minutes but not until doubled in volume. Brush the risen dough with the remaining glaze. Preheat oven to 375° F (190° C).

5. Bake in preheated oven for 40 to 45 minutes or until the stromboli sounds hollow when tapped on the bottom. Cool for 10 minutes before slicing to serve. Refrigerate leftovers.

K*eep this fat-free crisp on hand to serve to company as a snack with fresh vegetables. It's the perfect addition to a basket of soft rolls.*

Tip

Store in an airtight container and the lavosh will keep crisp for weeks.

To make sure the lavosh isn't tough, roll the dough as thinly as possible.

Variation

Any flavored olive oil can be used in this recipe. Try adding dried herbs (such as oregano, rosemary or thyme) to complement the oil.

Sun-Dried Tomato Lavosh

Makes 48 lavosh

Preheated baking stone or baking sheet

1 1/4 cups	water	300 mL
1/3 cup	sun-dried tomatoes, snipped into small pieces	75 mL
1 tsp	salt	5 mL
1 tsp	granulated sugar	5 mL
2 tbsp	roasted-garlic-and-basil flavored olive oil	25 mL
3 3/4 cups	bread flour	925 mL
2 tsp	dried basil	10 mL
1 tsp	bread machine yeast	5 mL
1 cup	grated Parmesan or aged Cheddar cheese	250 mL

1. Measure all ingredients *except cheese* into machine's baking pan in the order recommended by the manufacturer. Insert pan into the oven chamber. Select **Dough Cycle**.

2. Remove dough to a lightly floured surface. Cover with a large bowl and let rest for 10 to 15 minutes. Divide the dough into 4 portions. Sprinkle 1/4 cup (50 mL) of the cheese on the board. Place one portion of the dough on top of the cheese and roll as thinly as possible into a 7-inch (17.5 cm) wide rectangle, turning over frequently to press the cheese into the dough. With a pizza cutter or sharp knife, score into triangles with a base of 2 to 2 1/2 inches (5 to 6 cm), being careful not to cut all the way through. Repeat with remaining portions. Meanwhile, preheat oven to 375° F (190° C).

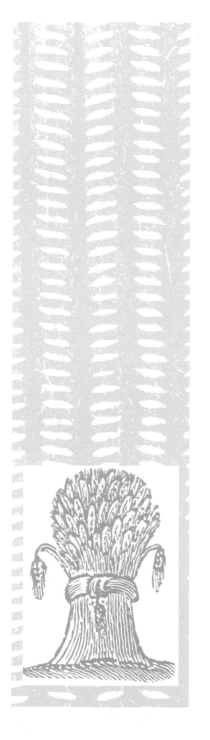

3. Place one rectangle at a time on prepared baking sheet or preheated baking stone. Bake in preheated oven for 13 to 18 minutes or until golden brown. Remove from oven and allow to cool. Break into long, thin triangles.

Y*ou and your guests will love this make-ahead luncheon entrée. Just add a salad to complete the menu.*

Tip

To boost the spiciness of this dish, add a small amount of Dijon mustard or Tabasco sauce to the filling.

Variation

Substitute your favorite fresh or dry herb for the savory. Ground beef, sausage or chicken can replace the turkey.

Turkey-Filled Cheese Braid

Makes 1 braid

Baking sheet, lightly greased

	Bread	
1 1/4 cups	water	300 mL
1 1/4 tsp	salt	6 mL
2 tbsp	granulated sugar	25 mL
1 tbsp	shortening	15 mL
3 3/4 cups	bread flour	925 mL
1/3 cup	buttermilk powder	75 mL
1/4 cup	grated Parmesan cheese	50 mL
1 1/2 tsp	bread machine yeast	7 mL

	Turkey Filling	
1 to 2 tbsp	vegetable oil	15 to 25 mL
1 lb	ground turkey, crumbled	500 g
1/2 cup	chopped onions	125 mL
1/3 cup	snipped fresh summer savory	75 mL
1 cup	grated aged Cheddar cheese	250 mL

1. Measure the bread ingredients into machine's baking pan in the order recommended by the manufacturer. Insert pan into the oven chamber. Select **Dough Cycle**.

2. Filling: In a large frying pan, heat oil over medium-high heat. Add turkey and cook until browned. Drain well, reserving drippings, and set turkey aside to cool. Return drippings to pan and add onions. Sauté until translucent; drain well. In a large bowl, combine turkey, onions, summer savory and Cheddar cheese. Mix well; set aside to cool.

3. Remove dough to a lightly floured surface. Cover with a large bowl and let rest for 10 to 15 minutes. Roll out the dough to a 20- by 15-inch (50 by 37.5 cm) rectangle. Cut into 3 strips, each 5 inches (12.5 cm) wide. Spread one-third of the filling down the center of each strip. Bring the edges together over the filling. Pinch to seal. Braid turkey-filled strips together and secure ends. Place on prepared baking sheet. Cover and let rise in a warm, draft-free place until doubled in volume. Meanwhile, preheat oven to 375° F (190° C).

4. Bake in preheated oven for 35 to 45 minutes or until braid sounds hollow when tapped on the bottom. Serve warm or cold.

*F*rom the Italian for *"old slipper," ciabatta are flat, chewy and fun to make. The specks of tomato provide bursts of flavor.*

Tip

To give a warm tomato color to the ciabatta, snip the sun-dried tomatoes into bite-size pieces before adding with the liquid. Use dry, not oil-packed, sun-dried tomatoes.

The dough should be slightly sticky — resist the temptation to add flour.

Dust the baking sheet and ciabatta with rice flour. It doesn't brown the way wheat flour does during baking.

Tomato Rosemary Ciabatta

Makes 2 ciabatta

Baking sheet, lightly floured

1 1/2 cups	water	375 mL
1/3 cup	sun-dried tomatoes, snipped into small pieces	75 mL
1 1/2 tsp	salt	7 mL
1 tsp	granulated sugar	5 mL
1 tbsp	olive oil	15 mL
1 1/4 cups	whole-wheat flour	300 mL
2 1/4 cups	bread flour	550 mL
1 tsp	dry rubbed rosemary	5 mL
1 1/2 tsp	bread machine yeast	7 mL

1. Measure all ingredients into machine's baking pan in the order recommended by the manufacturer. Insert pan into the oven chamber. Select **Dough Cycle**.

2. Remove dough to a lightly floured surface. Cover with a large bowl and let rest for 10 to 15 minutes. Divide the dough in half. Form each into a 13- by 4-inch (32.5 by 10 cm) oval. Place on prepared baking sheet. With floured fingers, make deep indentations all over each loaf making sure to press all the way down to the baking sheet. Dust the ovals lightly with flour. Cover and let rise in a warm, draft-free place for 30 to 45 minutes or until doubled in volume. Meanwhile, preheat oven to 425° F (220° C).

3. Make indents in the loaves a second time. Bake in preheated oven for 25 to 30 minutes or until ciabatta sound hollow when tapped on the bottom.

MORE FROM THE HEARTH

STEPS TO PERFECT ROLLS AND   58
HEARTH BREADS

12-GRAIN ROLLS   59

BONNIE'S APRÈS SKI LOAF   60

BRAIDED SQUASH CRESCENT   61

NEW ENGLAND MAPLE LEAF WALNUT LOAF   62

POTATO CLOVERLEAF ROLLS   63

MULTI-SEED BAGUETTES   64

SOUR CREAM PANSIES   65

TUSCAN WALNUT TOASTIES   66

TWISTED BREADSTICKS   68

WHEAT BERRY CROWN   69

WHOLE WHEAT ENGLISH MUFFINS   70

Straight from the hearth — for your family and friends.
Just try the delicious variety of shapes and textures.

STEPS TO PERFECT ROLLS AND HEARTH BREADS

1. Resting
Covering the dough and allowing it to rest relaxes the gluten. The result is dough that's less sticky, less resilient and easier to handle.

2. Shaping
If the dough cycle does not have an "add ingredients" signal, gently knead the fruit and nuts into the dough after it has rested (covered), for 10 to 15 minutes. Handle the dough as little as possible. The more flour added at this time, the tougher the finished product. Carefully follow the individual measuring instructions for each recipe. The baking times are based on specific sizes.

3. Proofing
Spray the dough lightly with vegetable spray, then cover it with waxed paper and a lint-free towel to keep it free from drafts. To test for readiness, press two fingers into the dough; the indents should remain.

4. Finishing
Make all slashes with a *lame* or a sharp knife (see entry for "slash" in Techniques Glossary, page 184). The deeper the cut, the wider it opens during baking. Brush the loaf lightly with egg wash or water, being careful not to deflate the loaf. Sprinkle with seeds or grains to add crunch.

5. Testing for doneness
Bread is baked when a metal-stemmed thermometer indicates an internal temperature of 190° F (95° C). The bread should sound hollow when tapped on the bottom. If the loaf is browning too quickly, cover loosely with foil.

*I*f you love hearty dinner
rolls, try these tonight.

Tip

If you've got some extra
wheat germ on hand, try
adding 1 to 2 tbsp (15 to
25 mL) to any bread, reducing the flour by an equal
amount. This won't affect the
shape of the loaf, and it's a
great way to add nutrients —
especially B-vitamins.

Variation

Substitute cracked wheat for
the 12-grain cereal.

Pan Rolls:

For a different kind of shape,
place the 12 balls of dough
in a lightly greased 8-inch
(2 L) square baking pan.
Cover and let rise in a warm,
draft-free place for 30 to
45 minutes or until doubled
in volume. Bake in preheated
oven for 30 to 45 minutes or
until rolls sound hollow when
tapped on the bottom.

12-Grain Rolls

Makes 12 rolls

Baking sheets, lightly greased

1 1/3 cups	water	325 mL
1 1/4 tsp	salt	6 mL
2 tbsp	honey	25 mL
2 tbsp	shortening	25 mL
1 1/2 cups	whole-wheat flour	375 mL
2 cups	bread flour	500 mL
3/4 cup	12-grain cereal	175 mL
2 tbsp	wheat germ	25 mL
2 tsp	bread machine yeast	10 mL

1. Measure ingredients into machine's baking pan in
   the order recommended by the manufacturer. Insert
   pan into the oven chamber. Select **Dough Cycle**.

2. Remove dough to a lightly floured surface. Cover
   with a large bowl and let rest for 10 to 15 minutes.
   Divide the dough in 12 portions. Roll into balls.
   Place balls on prepared baking sheets, setting them
   3 inches (7.5 cm) apart. Cover and let rise in a
   warm, draft-free place for 30 to 45 minutes or until
   doubled in volume. Meanwhile, preheat oven to
   375° F (190° C).

3. Bake in preheated oven for 15 to 20 minutes or until
   rolls sound hollow when tapped on the bottom.

Bonnie's Après Ski Loaf

*T*he perfect end to a day of skiing, serve this crunchy loaf with a bowl of spicy chili.

Tip

Substitute large-flake oatmeal or rye flakes for the barley flakes.

Variation

Instead of a single loaf, form dough into two narrow baguettes, each 14 inches (35 cm) long. Bake at 375° F (190° C) for 20 to 30 minutes. Slice on an angle.

Makes 1 loaf

Baking sheet, lightly greased

Bread

1 1/4 cups	water	300 mL
1/4 cup	nonfat dry milk	50 mL
1 1/2 tsp	salt	7 mL
3 tbsp	packed brown sugar	45 mL
2 tbsp	olive oil	25 mL
3 1/4 cups	bread flour	800 mL
2/3 cup	cracked wheat	150 mL
2/3 cup	barley flakes	150 mL
1/2 cup	raw unsalted sunflower seeds	125 mL
1 1/2 tsp	bread machine yeast	7 mL

Topping

2 tbsp	water	25 mL
2 to 3 tbsp	barley flakes	25 to 45 mL

1. Measure the bread ingredients into machine's baking pan in the order recommended by the manufacturer. Insert pan into the oven chamber. Select **Dough Cycle**.

2. Remove dough to a lightly floured surface. Cover with a large bowl and let rest for 10 to 15 minutes. Form into an Italian-style loaf, 12 by 4 inches (30 by 10 cm). Place on prepared baking sheet. Cover and let rise in a warm, draft-free place for 30 to 45 minutes or until doubled in volume. Meanwhile, preheat oven to 375° F (190° C).

3. Slash lengthwise, from end to end, 3/4 inch (2 cm) deep with a *lame* or sharp knife. Brush with the water and sprinkle with barley flakes. Bake in preheated oven for 30 to 35 minutes or until loaf sounds hollow when tapped on the bottom.

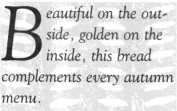

Beautiful on the outside, golden on the inside, this bread complements every autumn menu.

Tip

Use butternut or Hubbard squash for this recipe. Scoop out seeds from one half squash and cook in the microwave on High for 3 to 4 minutes per pound (500 g) or until tender, without adding butter or sugar.

For a light-textured loaf, mashed squash should be at room temperature before adding to baking pan.

Variation

Add 2/3 cup (150 mL) chopped pecans at the "add ingredient" signal or knead into the dough after resting, before forming into ropes.

Braided Squash Crescent

Makes 1 crescent

Baking sheet, lightly greased

Bread

1/2 cup	water	125 mL
1 cup	mashed cooked squash	50 mL
1	egg	1
1/4 cup	nonfat dry milk	50 mL
1 1/2 tsp	salt	7 mL
3 tbsp	packed brown sugar	45 mL
2 tbsp	butter	25 mL
3 3/4 cups	bread flour	925 mL
1/2 tsp	ground nutmeg	2 mL
1 1/2 tsp	bread machine yeast	7 mL

Seed Glaze

1	egg yolk	1
1 tbsp	water	15 mL
2 tbsp	sunflower or sesame seeds	25 mL

1. Measure the bread ingredients into machine's baking pan in the order recommended by the manufacturer. Insert pan into the oven chamber. Select **Dough Cycle**.

2. Remove dough to a lightly floured surface. Cover with a large bowl and let rest for 10 to 15 minutes. Divide dough into 3 portions. Roll each, with the palm of your hand, into a long smooth rope, 1 inch (2.5 cm) in diameter. Taper at ends, leaving the middle thicker. Braid the 3 ropes and place on prepared baking sheet, curving to form a crescent. Cover and let rise in a warm, draft-free place for 30 to 45 minutes or until doubled in volume. Meanwhile, preheat oven to 350° F (180° C).

3. In a small bowl, whisk together egg yolk and water until smooth. Brush the risen dough lightly with glaze and sprinkle with seeds. Bake in preheated oven for 25 to 30 minutes or until crescent sounds hollow when tapped on the bottom.

W*hat a way to celebrate Independence Day! Take this loaf to your family picnic and listen to the raves.*

Tip

To make a leaf pattern for dusting: Draw one half of a maple leaf on a folded piece of paper, cut it out and unfold for a symmetrical leaf. Make your pattern the size just to fit the flat top of the loaf. Be sure to dust with rice flour, since it does not brown during baking.

Variation

To bake this dough in your machine, prepare on a 2 lb (1 kg) **Basic Cycle**.

New England Maple Leaf Walnut Loaf

Makes 1 loaf

Baking sheet, lightly greased

1 1/4 cups	water	300 mL
2 tsp	maple flavoring	10 mL
1/4 cup	nonfat dry milk	50 mL
1 1/2 tsp	salt	7 mL
2 tbsp	maple syrup	25 mL
2 tbsp	packed brown sugar	25 mL
2 tbsp	butter	25 mL
3 1/2 cups	bread flour	875 mL
1 cup	chopped walnuts	250 mL
1 1/2 tsp	bread machine yeast	7 mL
	Rice flour	

1. Measure ingredients *except rice flour* into machine's baking pan in the order recommended by the manufacturer. Insert pan into the oven chamber. Select **Dough Cycle**.

2. Remove dough to a lightly floured surface. Cover with a large bowl and let rest for 10 to 15 minutes. Form dough into a large oval or round, flattening the top slightly. Place on prepared baking sheet. Gently place a real maple leaf or maple leaf pattern on top of the center of the loaf. Dust around the leaf generously with rice flour. Remove leaf, being careful not to get flour on the center of the loaf. Cover and let rise in a warm, draft-free place for 30 to 45 minutes or until doubled in volume. Meanwhile, preheat oven to 350° F (180° C).

3. Bake in preheated oven for 35 to 40 minutes or until loaf sounds hollow when tapped on the bottom.

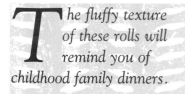

he fluffy texture of these rolls will remind you of childhood family dinners.

Tip

Bake an extra potato or use leftover baked potatoes. Simply peel and mash quickly with a fork. No need to add any butter or salt. One large potato makes 3/4 cup (175 mL) mashed.

Variation

To make this recipe as a loaf, select the 2 lb (1 kg) **Basic Cycle** rather than the **Dough Cycle**.

Potato Cloverleaf Rolls

Makes 18 rolls

Muffin tins, lightly greased

1 1/3 cups	water	325 mL
1/4 cup	nonfat dry milk	50 mL
1 1/2 tsp	salt	7 mL
1 tbsp	packed brown sugar	15 mL
2 tbsp	butter	25 mL
4 1/4 cups	bread flour	1050 mL
3/4 cup	mashed baked potato	175 mL
1 tsp	dried thyme	5 mL
1	clove garlic, minced	1
1 3/4 tsp	bread machine yeast	8 mL

1. Measure ingredients into machine's baking pan in the order recommended by the manufacturer. Insert pan into the oven chamber. Select **Dough Cycle**.

2. Remove dough to a lightly floured surface. Cover with a large bowl and let rest for 10 to 15 minutes. Divide the dough into 54 portions. Roll into balls. Place 3 balls in each cup of prepared muffin tins. Cover and let rise in a warm, draft-free place for 30 to 45 minutes or until doubled in volume. Meanwhile, preheat oven to 350° F (180° C).

3. Bake in preheated oven for 15 to 20 minutes or until rolls sound hollow when tapped on the bottom.

*W*ith its hearty combination of cracked wheat, flaxseeds and sunflower seeds, this loaf is equally good with a comforting winter stew or a crisp summer salad.

Tip

Be patient! This heavier-textured loaf may take a little longer to double in volume.

Variation

Seed Glaze: Before rising and baking, brush the top of the baguettes with water and roll in sunflower seeds or a mixture of flaxseeds and sunflower seeds. The flavor of the roasted seeds is delicious and the top crust turns a crispy, golden brown.

Multi-Seed Baguettes

Makes 2 baguettes

Baking sheet, lightly greased

1 1/2 cups	water	375 mL
1 1/2 tsp	salt	7 mL
1 tbsp	packed brown sugar	15 mL
2 tbsp	shortening	25 mL
1 1/2 cups	whole-wheat flour	375 mL
1 3/4 cups	bread flour	425 mL
1/2 cup	cracked wheat	125 mL
1/4 cup	flaxseeds	50 mL
1/4 cup	sunflower seeds	50 mL
2 1/4 tsp	bread machine yeast	11 mL

1. Measure ingredients into machine's baking pan in the order recommended by the manufacturer. Insert pan into the oven chamber. Select **Dough Cycle**.

2. Remove dough to a lightly floured surface. Cover with a large bowl and let rest for 10 to 15 minutes. Divide dough in half. Form each half into a 16-inch (40 cm) stick, 1 inch (2.5 cm) in diameter. Place on prepared baking sheet. Cover and let rise in a warm, draft-free place for 30 to 45 minutes or until doubled in volume. Meanwhile, preheat oven to 400° F (200° C).

3. With a *lame* or a sharp knife, gently cut 5 long parallel diagonal slashes approximately 1/2 inch (1 cm) deep across the top of risen loaves. Spritz with cold water just before baking. Spritz 3 to 4 times during first 5 minutes of baking. Bake in preheated oven for 20 to 25 minutes or until baguettes sound hollow when tapped on the bottom.

SAUSAGE-STUFFED STROMBOLI (PAGE 50) ➤

OVERLEAF (FROM LEFT): IRISH FRECKLE BREAD (PAGE 122);
CHRISTINE'S FRUITED PUMPERNICKEL (PAGE 18);
BROWN SEED BREAD (PAGE 75); PUMPERNICKEL TURBAN (PAGE 140)

A rich, creamy crust and an interesting shape. These pansies are delicious — and fun, too!

Tip

Be sure to make the cuts deep enough, or the shape of the petals will be lost when the dough rises.

Variation

Think of any large-petalled flower and make the number of cuts needed to recreate the appearance you want.

Sour Cream Pansies

Makes 16 pansies

Baking sheet, lightly greased

Bread

1/2 cup	water	125 mL
1/2 cup	sour cream	125 mL
2	eggs	2
1 1/4 tsp	salt	6 mL
2 tbsp	granulated sugar	25 mL
2 tbsp	butter	25 mL
3 1/4 cups	bread flour	800 mL
1 1/2 tsp	bread machine yeast	7 mL

Glaze

1	egg yolk	1
1 tbsp	water	15 mL
2 tbsp	sesame or poppy seeds	25 mL

1. Measure bread ingredients into machine's baking pan in the order recommended by the manufacturer. Insert pan into the oven chamber. Select **Dough Cycle**.

2. Remove dough to a lightly floured surface. Cover with a large bowl and let rest for 10 to 15 minutes. Divide the dough into 16 portions. Roll into balls and place on prepared baking sheet; flatten tops slightly. Using kitchen shears, make 5 cuts, each 1/2 inch (1 cm) long, all the way through the dough, equally spaced around the outside. Cover and let rise in a warm, draft-free place for 30 to 45 minutes or until doubled in volume. Meanwhile, preheat oven to 375° F (190° C).

3. Glaze: In a small bowl, whisk together egg yolk and water until smooth. Brush the risen dough with the glaze. Sprinkle the center of each pansy with seeds. Bake in preheated oven for 15 to 20 minutes or until pansies sound hollow when tapped on the bottom.

≺ BRAIDED SQUASH CRESCENT (PAGE 61)

Try these sandwiches (great for take-out lunches!) and you'll understand the Tuscan attitude to food: "with love, from the heart."

Tip

Feel free to use your own favorite sandwich fillings.

Tuscan Walnut Toasties

Makes 1 or 2 toasties

Baking sheet, lightly greased

Bread

1 1/2 cups	water	375 mL
1 tsp	orange zest	5 mL
1 1/2 tsp	salt	7 mL
1 tbsp	granulated sugar	15 mL
3 3/4 cups	bread flour	950 mL
1/3 cup	buttermilk powder	75 mL
2/3 cup	chopped walnuts	150 mL
2 tsp	bread machine yeast	10 mL

Sandwich Filling

	Lean prosciutto, thinly sliced	
	Genoa salami, thinly sliced	
	Provolone or Monterey Jack cheese, thinly sliced	
1/2 cup	alfalfa sprouts	125 mL
2 tbsp	extra virgin olive oil	25 mL

1. Measure ingredients into machine's baking pan in the order recommended by the manufacturer. Insert pan into the oven chamber. Select **Dough Cycle**.

2. Remove dough to a lightly floured surface. Cover with a large bowl and let rest for 10 to 15 minutes. Form into one 9-inch (22.5 cm) loaf or two 6-inch (15 cm) round loaves with slightly flattened tops. Place on prepared baking sheet. Using a pizza wheel, cut into 6 or 8 wedges. Cover and let rise in a warm, draft-free place for 30 to 45 minutes or until doubled in volume. Meanwhile, preheat oven to 375° F (190° C).

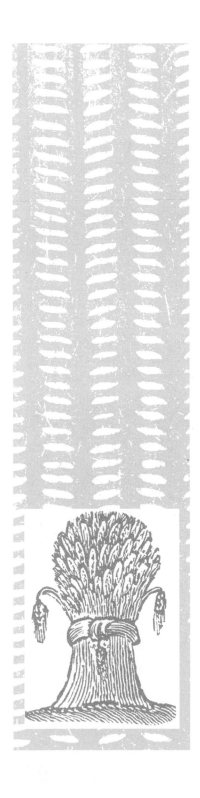

3. Bake in preheated oven for 25 to 40 minutes or until loaves sound hollow when tapped on the bottom. Set aside to cool completely.

4. Preheat barbecue or grill. Slice each baked toastie in half horizontally. On the bottom half, arrange prosciutto, salami, cheese and alfalfa sprouts. Top with other half of toastie and press together. Brush both sides of sandwiches with a thin layer of oil before placing on hot barbecue or grill. Cook, turning once, until the sandwich is browned, crisp and the cheese is melted. Cut into wedges. Serve hot.

*M*ake these bread-
sticks at home
and serve them
as Italian restaurants do —
with a dish of flavored olive
oil for dipping.

Tip

For thinner, crunchier breadsticks, do not let the dough
rise; bake immediately.

Variation

Brush with an egg white
glaze and sprinkle with
freshly grated Parmesan
(or your favorite dried herbs)
just before baking.

Twisted Breadsticks

Makes 12 breadsticks

Baking sheet, lightly greased

1 1/3 cups	water	325 mL
1 1/2 tsp	salt	7 mL
1 tbsp	granulated sugar	15 mL
1 tbsp	vegetable oil	15 mL
3 1/2 cups	bread flour	875 mL
1/3 cup	buttermilk powder	75 mL
1 1/4 tsp	bread machine yeast	6 mL

1. Measure ingredients into machine's baking pan in the order recommended by the manufacturer. Insert pan into the oven chamber. Select **Dough Cycle**.

2. Remove dough to a lightly floured surface. Cover with a large bowl and let rest for 10 to 15 minutes. Roll out dough into a 16- by 6-inch (40 by 15 cm) rectangle. Cut into 12 strips, each 16 inches (40 cm) long and 1/2 inch (1 cm) wide. Fold strips in half lengthwise to 8 inches (20 cm) in length.

3. Place one strip crosswise on the surface in front of you. With the palm of your hands, roll one end towards you and the other end away from you so that the strip twists. Stretch the strip slightly as you twist it. Repeat with remaining strips. Place on prepared baking sheet. Cover and let rise in a warm, draft-free place for 30 to 45 minutes or until doubled in volume. Meanwhile, preheat oven to 400° F (200° C).

4. Bake in preheated oven for 15 to 18 minutes or until breadsticks sound hollow when tapped.

Here's flavor fit for a king (or queen). The cooked wheat berries and sunflower seeds add extra crunch.

Tip

Make cuts deep enough to get the full effect of the crown shape.

For instructions on cooking wheat berries, see Techniques Glossary, page 183.

Variation

Substitute cooked rye berries or bulgur for the wheat berries.

Wheat Berry Crown

Makes 1 loaf

Baking sheet, lightly greased

1 1/3 cups	water	325 mL
1 1/2 tsp	salt	7 mL
3 tbsp	packed brown sugar	45 mL
2 tbsp	vegetable oil	25 mL
2 cups	whole-wheat flour	500 mL
1 1/2 cups	bread flour	375 mL
1/3 cup	buttermilk powder	75 mL
1/2 cup	raw unsalted sunflower seeds	125 mL
1/3 cup	cooked wheat berries	75 mL
1 1/2 tsp	bread machine yeast	7 mL

1. Measure ingredients into machine's baking pan in the order recommended by the manufacturer. Insert pan into the oven chamber. Select **Dough Cycle**.

2. Remove dough to a lightly floured surface. Cover with a large bowl and let rest for 10 to 15 minutes. Form into a high round ball. Place on prepared baking sheet. Cover and let rise in a warm, draft-free place for 30 to 45 minutes or until doubled in volume. Meanwhile, set oven rack to lowest position in oven. Pre-heat oven to 425° F (220° C).

3. With a sharp knife or *lame*, gently cut 4 intersecting slashes, each 3/4 inch (2 cm) deep, across top of ball. Bake in preheated oven for 10 minutes. Reduce oven temperature to 375° F (190° C) and bake for 30 to 40 minutes or until crown sounds hollow when tapped on the bottom.

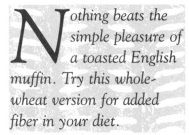

Nothing beats the simple pleasure of a toasted English muffin. Try this whole-wheat version for added fiber in your diet.

Tip

Make sure English muffins are not too thick or they will burn on the outside before cooking through to the center.

The slight indent on the sides of the English muffin makes a perfect place to split with a fork before toasting.

Whole Wheat English Muffins

Makes 18 muffins

Baking sheet, sprinkled with cornmeal

Muffin

1 cup	milk	250 mL
2	eggs	2
1 tsp	salt	5 mL
1 tbsp	honey	15 mL
1 tbsp	molasses	15 mL
2 tbsp	shortening	25 mL
2 cups	whole-wheat flour	500 mL
1 1/2 cups	bread flour	375 mL
1 1/4 tsp	bread machine yeast	6 mL
2 to 3 tbsp	cornmeal	25 to 45 mL

Orange Honey Butter

1/3 cup	soft butter	75 mL
2 tbsp	creamed honey	25 mL
1 tsp	orange zest	5 mL

1. Measure muffin ingredients, *except the cornmeal*, into machine's baking pan in the order recommended by the manufacturer. Insert pan into the oven chamber. Select **Dough Cycle**.

2. Remove dough to a lightly floured surface. Cover with a large bowl and let rest for 10 to 15 minutes. Roll out the dough to 1/4-inch (5 mm) thickness. Cut into 3-inch (7.5 cm) circles. Place on prepared baking sheet. Brush with water and sprinkle tops with cornmeal. Cover and let rise in a warm, draft-free place for 30 to 45 minutes or until doubled in volume.

3. Preheat grill to 500° F (260° C). Grill muffins for 6 to 7 minutes per side or until golden.

4. Honey Butter: In a small bowl, cream together butter, honey and orange zest. Spread on toasted English muffins. Store in refrigerator if not using immediately; warm to room temperature before spreading.

SEEDS AND NUTS

THE FAT/FIBER CONNECTION 72

ALMOND APRICOT YOGURT BREAD 73

AMISH SEED BREAD 74

BROWN SEED BREAD 75

HONEY BERRY SEED BREAD 76

JAVA CHOCOLATE CRUNCH LOAF 77

MAPLE BANANA FLAXSEED BREAD 78

PEANUT RYE LOAF 80

POPPY THYME BREAD 81

TRAIL BREAD 82

Enjoy the extra crunch of nutritious grains and seeds in these healthy breads and loaves.

The fat/fiber connection

Breads containing seeds and nuts have multiple health benefits. They contain heart-healthy fats such as omega-3, as well as different types of fiber and other nutritious compounds.

To lower the fat and increase the fiber in breads, make substitutions based on the values given below.

	Fat (g)	Fiber (g)
Seeds (1 cup [250 mL])		
Caraway	1	3
Flaxseed(s)	52	43
Poppy	4	1
Pumpkin	63	5
Sesame	71	17
Sunflower	63	14
Nuts (1 cup [250 mL])		
Almonds	70	15
Hazelnuts (Filberts)	70	11
Pecans	86	11
Pistachios	55	12
Walnuts	76	4

*W*ith its flecks of golden apricots, this sweet bread is a treat for the eye — and tastebuds! Serve it with fresh fruit for a late Sunday brunch.

Tip

Use scissors to snip dried apricots into 6 pieces.

For instructions on toasting almonds, see Techniques Glossary, page 183.

The recipe was developed using both apricot- and peach-flavored yogurt — in regular, low-fat and fat-free varieties. Each type resulted in a slightly different bread, but they all tasted great.

Almond Apricot Yogurt Bread

1.5 LB (750 G)

1/2 cup	water	125 mL
1/2 cup	fruit-flavored yogurt (see note, at left)	125 mL
1	egg	1
1 1/4 tsp	salt	6 mL
2 tbsp	granulated sugar	25 mL
2 tbsp	butter	25 mL
2 1/2 cups	bread flour	625 mL
1 tsp	ground nutmeg	5 mL
1 1/2 tsp	bread machine yeast	7 mL
2/3 cup	slivered toasted almonds	150 mL
2/3 cup	snipped dried apricots	150 mL

2 LB (1 KG)　　　　　　　　　　　　　　　　　　**L**

3/4 cup	water	175 mL
1/2 cup	fruit-flavored yogurt (see note, at left)	125 mL
1	egg	1
1 1/2 tsp	salt	7 mL
2 tbsp	granulated sugar	25 mL
2 tbsp	butter	25 mL
3 1/4 cups	bread flour	800 mL
1 1/2 tsp	ground nutmeg	7 mL
2 tsp	bread machine yeast	10 mL
3/4 cup	slivered toasted almonds	175 mL
3/4 cup	snipped dried apricots	175 mL

1. Measure all ingredients *except almonds and dried apricots* into baking pan in the order recommended by the manufacturer. Insert pan into the oven chamber. Select **Sweet Cycle**. Add almonds and dried apricots at "add ingredient" cycle.

W*ith its rough top studded by sesame seeds, this loaf has a heavier texture than most. Its sharp, sourdough-like taste is deliciously distinctive — but may not appeal to everyone.*

Tip

For a lighter texture, substitute 1 cup (250 mL) bread flour for 1 cup (250 mL) of the whole-wheat flour.

Variation

Use any flavor of liquid honey. Orange-blossom or clover honey will produce a milder-flavored loaf than buckwheat.

Amish Seed Bread

1.5 LB (750 G)

1/4 cup	water	50 mL
3/4 cup	plain yogurt	175 mL
1	egg	1
1 1/4 tsp	salt	6 mL
3 tbsp	buckwheat honey	45 mL
1 tbsp	shortening	15 mL
1 1/2 cups	whole-wheat flour	375 mL
1 cup	bread flour	250 mL
1/3 cup	quick-cooking oats	75 mL
3 tbsp	wheat bran	45 mL
3 tbsp	sesame seeds	45 mL
1 3/4 tsp	bread machine yeast	8 mL

2 LB (1 KG)

1/2 cup	water	125 mL
1 cup	plain yogurt	250 mL
1	egg	1
1 1/4 tsp	salt	6 mL
1/4 cup	buckwheat honey	50 mL
1 tbsp	shortening	15 mL
1 3/4 cups	whole-wheat flour	425 mL
1 3/4 cups	bread flour	425 mL
1/2 cup	quick-cooking oats	125 mL
1/4 cup	wheat bran	50 mL
1/4 cup	sesame seeds	50 mL
2 tsp	bread machine yeast	10 mL

1. Measure ingredients into baking pan in the order recommended by the manufacturer. Insert pan into the oven chamber. Select **Whole Wheat Cycle.**

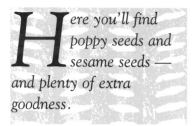

Here you'll find poppy seeds and sesame seeds — and plenty of extra goodness.

Tip

To get the quantity exactly right, add the amount of water called for to a 2-cup (500 mL) glass measure. Then add the cottage cheese until the level reaches the correct total volume of both ingredients.

Yes, you're reading it right: The 1.5 lb (750 g) recipe contains the *same* amount of yeast as the 2 lb (1 kg).

Variation

Substituting ricotta cheese for the cottage cheese gives a slightly creamier texture.

Brown Seed Bread

1.5 LB (750 G)

1 cup	water	250 mL
1/2 cup	cottage cheese	125 mL
1 1/2 tsp	salt	7 mL
1/4 cup	honey	50 mL
2 tbsp	shortening	25 mL
1 1/2 cups	whole-wheat flour	375 mL
1 1/2 cups	bread flour	375 mL
1/2 cup	barley flakes	125 mL
1/2 cup	bran cereal	125 mL
1/4 cup	poppy seeds	50 mL
1/4 cup	sesame seeds	50 mL
1 3/4 tsp	bread machine yeast	8 mL

2 LB (1 KG)

1 1/4 cups	water	300 mL
3/4 cup	cottage cheese	175 mL
1 3/4 tsp	salt	8 mL
1/3 cup	honey	75 mL
3 tbsp	shortening	45 mL
2 cups	whole-wheat flour	500 mL
2 cups	bread flour	500 mL
1/2 cup	barley flakes	125 mL
1/2 cup	bran cereal	125 mL
1/3 cup	poppy seeds	75 mL
1/3 cup	sesame seeds	75 mL
1 3/4 tsp	bread machine yeast	8 mL

1. Measure ingredients into baking pan in the order recommended by the manufacturer. Insert pan into the oven chamber. Select **Whole Wheat Cycle**.

W*e held a contest among our newsletter readers to name this bread. The winning entry came from Sue Phillips of Sorrento, B.C., who was inspired by the "very delightful taste of honey, wheat berries and a combination of sesame, sunflower and poppy seeds — a real comfort food!"*

Tip

For instructions on cooking wheat berries, see Techniques Glossary, page 183.

Cook enough wheat berries for several loaves. Store in the refrigerator in an airtight container for 3 to 4 weeks.

Variation

Substitute cracked wheat or bulgur for the wheat berries.

Honey Berry Seed Bread

1.5 LB (750 G)

1 1/4 cups	water	300 mL
1 1/2 tsp	salt	7 mL
2 tbsp	honey	25 mL
2 tbsp	shortening	25 mL
1 cup	whole-wheat flour	250 mL
1 3/4 cups	bread flour	425 mL
1/3 cup	buttermilk powder	75 mL
1/3 cup	cooked wheat berries	75 mL
1/4 cup	sesame seeds	50 mL
1/4 cup	raw unsalted sunflower seeds	50 mL
1/4 cup	poppy seeds	50 mL
1 tsp	bread machine yeast	5 mL

2 LB (1 KG)

1 1/3 cups	water	325 mL
1 1/2 tsp	salt	7 mL
3 tbsp	honey	45 mL
2 tbsp	shortening	25 mL
1 1/4 cups	whole-wheat flour	300 mL
1 3/4 cups	bread flour	425 mL
1/2 cup	buttermilk powder	125 mL
1/2 cup	cooked wheat berries	125 mL
1/3 cup	sesame seeds	75 mL
1/3 cup	raw unsalted sunflower seeds	75 mL
1/4 cup	poppy seeds	50 mL
1 1/2 tsp	bread machine yeast	7 mL

1. Measure ingredients into baking pan in the order recommended by the manufacturer. Insert pan into the oven chamber. Select **Whole Wheat Cycle**.

*S*erved with fresh strawberries, this coffee-chocolate dessert bread is ideal for a bridal shower.

Tip

Chances are you'll have to shell the pistachio nuts yourself. But if you can find pre-shelled nuts, use them — you'll save a lot of time.

Yes, you're reading it right: The 1.5 lb (750 g) recipe contains *more* yeast than the 2 lb (1 kg).

Variation

Substitute espresso coffee for the regular brewed.

Java Chocolate Crunch Loaf

1.5 LB (750 G)

3/4 cup	water	175 mL
1/3 cup	lukewarm coffee	75 mL
1/4 cup	nonfat dry milk	50 mL
1 1/4 tsp	salt	6 mL
2 tbsp	honey	25 mL
2 tbsp	vegetable oil	25 mL
3 1/4 cups	bread flour	800 mL
1 tbsp	unsweetened cocoa	15 mL
1/3 cup	pistachio nuts	75 mL
1 1/2 tsp	bread machine yeast	7 mL

2 LB (1 KG)

1 cup	water	250 mL
1/2 cup	lukewarm coffee	125 mL
1/3 cup	nonfat dry milk	75 mL
1 1/2 tsp	salt	7 mL
2 tbsp	honey	25 mL
2 tbsp	vegetable oil	25 mL
4 cups	bread flour	1000 mL
2 tbsp	unsweetened cocoa	25 mL
1/2 cup	pistachio nuts	125 mL
1 1/4 tsp	bread machine yeast	5 mL

1. Measure all ingredients into baking pan in the order recommended by the manufacturer. Insert pan into the oven chamber. Select **Sweet Cycle**.

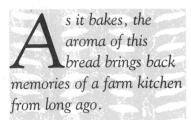

As it bakes, the aroma of this bread brings back memories of a farm kitchen from long ago.

Tip

Mash and freeze ripe bananas so they're ready when you need them. Thaw and warm to room temperature before using.

Yes, you're reading it right: The 1.5 lb (750 g) recipe contains the *same* amount of yeast as the 2 lb (1 kg).

Variation

Light or regular pancake syrup, or honey, can be substituted for the maple syrup.

Maple Banana Flaxseed Bread

1.5 LB (750 G)

1/3 cup	water	75 mL
1 cup	mashed bananas	250 mL
1/4 cup	nonfat dry milk	50 mL
1 1/2 tsp	salt	7 mL
2 tbsp	maple syrup	25 mL
2 tbsp	shortening	25 mL
3/4 cup	whole-wheat flour	175 mL
2 cups	bread flour	500 mL
1/4 cup	flaxseeds	50 mL
1/4 cup	chopped walnuts	50 mL
1/2 tsp	cinnamon	2 mL
1/4 tsp	ground ginger	1 mL
1 1/2 tsp	bread machine yeast	7 mL

2 LB (1 KG)

1/2 cup	water	125 mL
1 cup	mashed bananas	250 mL
1/3 cup	nonfat dry milk	75 mL
1 1/2 tsp	salt	7 mL
3 tbsp	maple syrup	45 mL
2 tbsp	shortening	25 mL
1 cup	whole-wheat flour	250 mL
2 1/4 cups	bread flour	550 mL
1/3 cup	flaxseeds	75 mL
1/3 cup	chopped walnuts	75 mL
1/2 tsp	cinnamon	2 mL
1/4 tsp	ground ginger	1 mL
1 1/2 tsp	bread machine yeast	7 mL

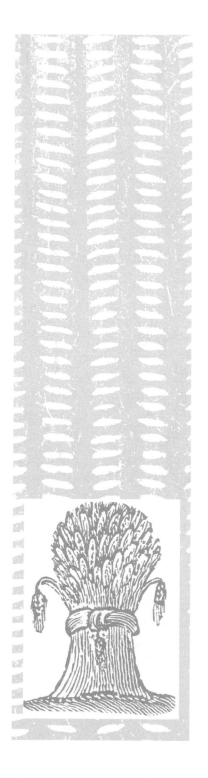

1. Measure ingredients into baking pan in the order recommended by the manufacturer. Insert pan into the oven chamber. Select **Whole Wheat Cycle**

This sensational flavor combination was inspired by a recipe for peanut butter rye cookies. It works even better as a bread — partic- ularly with the surprising extra crunch of peanuts baked right into the loaf.

Tip

Rye flour is much lower in gluten than wheat flour, so this loaf is quite compact.

Use either smooth or crunchy peanut butter.

The peanuts can be added directly with the flour; no need to wait for the "add ingredient" signal.

Peanut Rye Loaf

1.5 LB (750 G)

1 1/2 cups	water	375 mL
1/4 cup	nonfat dry milk	50 mL
1 1/2 tsp	salt	7 mL
2 tbsp	packed brown sugar	25 mL
2 tbsp	peanut butter	25 mL
3 cups	bread flour	750 mL
3/4 cup	rye flour	175 mL
2/3 cup	unsalted peanuts	150 mL
1 tsp	bread machine yeast	5 mL

2 LB (1 KG)   L

1 2/3 cups	water	400 mL
1/3 cup	nonfat dry milk	75 mL
1 1/2 tsp	salt	7 mL
3 tbsp	packed brown sugar	45 mL
3 tbsp	peanut butter	45 mL
4 cups	bread flour	1000 mL
3/4 cup	rye flour	175 mL
3/4 cup	unsalted peanuts	175 mL
1 1/4 tsp	bread machine yeast	5 mL

1. Measure ingredients into baking pan in the order recommended by the manufacturer. Insert pan into the oven chamber. Select **Basic Cycle**.

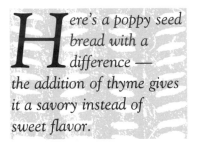

ere's a poppy seed bread with a difference — the addition of thyme gives it a savory instead of sweet flavor.

Tip

If using fresh thyme, wash and dry well before snipping with kitchen shears or sharp scissors.

Variation

Substitute an equal quantity of marjoram for the thyme.

Poppy Thyme Bread

1.5 LB (750 G)

3/4 cup	water	175 mL
2	eggs	2
1 1/4 tsp	salt	6 mL
2 tbsp	honey	25 mL
2 tbsp	butter	25 mL
2 2/3 cups	bread flour	650 mL
1/4 cup	poppy seeds	50 mL
1 tsp	dried thyme (or 1 tbsp [15 mL] snipped fresh thyme)	5 mL
3/4 tsp	bread machine yeast	3 mL

2 LB (1 KG)

1 cup	water	250 mL
2	eggs	2
1 1/4 tsp	salt	6 mL
2 tbsp	honey	25 mL
2 tbsp	butter	25 mL
4 cups	bread flour	1000 mL
1/3 cup	poppy seeds	75 mL
1 1/2 tsp	dried thyme (or 2 tbsp [25 mL] snipped fresh thyme)	7 mL
1 tsp	bread machine yeast	5 mL

1. Measure ingredients into baking pan in the order recommended by the manufacturer. Insert pan into the oven chamber. Select **Basic Cycle**.

The tang of yogurt enhances the mix of fruits in this bread, while the nuts provide a delightful crunch.

Tip

Different types of trail mix will affect the taste and appearance of this bread. Try making it with Sierra, Harvest or Manhattan Mix.

Yes, you're reading it right: The 1.5 lb (750 g) recipe contains the *same* amount of yeast as the 2 lb (1 kg).

Trail Bread

1.5 LB (750 G)

1/2 cup	water	125 mL
3/4 cup	fruit-flavored yogurt	175 mL
1 tsp	salt	5 mL
3 tbsp	granulated sugar	45 mL
1 tbsp	shortening	15 mL
2 3/4 cups	bread flour	675 mL
3/4 cup	trail mix (see note, at left)	175 mL
1 1/2 tsp	bread machine yeast	7 mL

2 LB (1 KG) Ⓛ

1 cup	water	250 mL
3/4 cup	fruit-flavored yogurt	175 mL
1 1/2 tsp	salt	7 mL
3 tbsp	granulated sugar	45 mL
2 tbsp	shortening	25 mL
3 3/4 cups	bread flour	925 mL
1 1/2 cups	trail mix (see note, at left)	375 mL
1 1/2 tsp	bread machine yeast	7 mL

1. Measure ingredients into baking pan in the the order recommended by the manufacturer. Insert pan into the oven chamber. Select **Sweet Cycle**.

MORE BAGELS AND SOURDOUGHS

BAGEL-MAKING TIPS   84

BASIC BAGELS   85

CINNAMON RAISIN BAGELS   86

MULTIGRAIN BAGELS   87

NEW BEGINNINGS FOR SOURDOUGH:
   STARTERS VS. SOURS   88

BASIC SOUR MIX   89

TIPS FOR WORKING WITH SOURDOUGH   90

FRENCH WALNUT RAISIN SOURDOUGH   91

ONION CHEDDAR SOURDOUGH   92
   HAMBURGER BUNS

SOURDOUGH BAGUETTES   93

SOURDOUGH BOULE   94

Bagels and sourdoughs present more of a challenge than basic bread recipes, but the results are well worth the extra effort.

BAGEL-MAKING TIPS

• Use the **Dough Cycle** of your bread machine, but only for the kneading portion of the cycle. Remove the dough as soon as kneading finishes; do not allow it to remain in the bread machine to rise and finish the cycle. By doing this, you will end up with a more bagel-like appearance and texture. To get an idea of how long the kneading portion is, check the user's manual for your bread machine.

• Boiling bagels before baking gives them a shiny appearance, thick crust and characteristically chewy texture.

Boiling deactivates the yeast by raising the internal temperature to 130° F (55° C). Just be sure that you don't boil longer than the time stated in the recipe or the result will be small, tough bagels.

• Sprinkling the baking sheet with cornmeal or semolina flour (rather than greasing it) results in a more authentic bagel. For a crunchy finish, dip bagels quickly into a small bowl of seeds before baking.

*L*ike most bagels today, these are doughnut-shaped. But the first bagels — thought to have originated from Poland in the late 1600's — were made in the shape of a horse's stirrup.

Tip

There are several methods used to form bagels, but we recommend the "cylinder method" described here. It's almost foolproof!

Variation

Use your bagels to make bagel chips. To learn how, see Techniques Glossary, page 183.

Basic Bagels

Makes 9 bagels

Baking sheet, lightly greased
Preheated baking stone (optional)

1 1/4 cups	water	300 mL
1 tsp	salt	5 mL
2 tbsp	honey	25 mL
4 cups	bread flour	1000 mL
1 3/4 tsp	bread machine yeast	8 mL
1 tbsp	granulated sugar	15 mL

1. Measure all ingredients *except granulated sugar* into machine's baking pan in the order recommended by the manufacturer. Insert pan into the oven chamber. Select **Dough Cycle**.

2. Stop bread machine when the kneading portion of the cycle is complete. (Do not allow dough to rise in the machine.) Remove dough to a lightly floured surface. Cover with a large bowl and let rest for 10 to 15 minutes. Shape the dough into a round cylinder 13 1/2 inches (36 cm) long. Cut into 9 equal slices, each 1 1/2 inches (4 cm) thick. Push thumbs through the center of each slice and pull into a bagel shape, rounding all surfaces. Place on prepared baking sheet. Cover and let rise in a warm, draft-free place for 15 to 20 minutes. Meanwhile, preheat oven to 400° F (200° C).

3. Bring a large pot of water to a gentle (but full) boil; add sugar. Immerse bagels one at a time in boiling water, turning upside down. With a skimmer or large spoon, hold bagel under the water for 20 seconds or until the dough becomes a little puffy. Place on prepared baking sheet or on preheated baking stone. Bake in preheated oven for 15 to 20 minutes or until bagels sound hollow when tapped on the bottom.

*P*erfect for breakfast or a mid-morning snack, these bagels are delicious toasted and spread with cream cheese.

Tip

Turning the bagel upside-down during boiling helps to ensure a rounded top.

Variation

Substitute dried cranberries for the raisins and cardamom for the cinnamon.

Cinnamon Raisin Bagels

Makes 9 bagels

Baking sheet, lightly greased
Preheated baking stone (optional)

1 1/2 cups	water	375 mL
1 tsp	salt	5 mL
3 tbsp	packed brown sugar	45 mL
1 1/2 cups	whole-wheat flour	375 mL
2 3/4 cups	bread flour	675 mL
1 tsp	ground cinnamon	5 mL
2 tsp	bread machine yeast	10 mL
3/4 cup	raisins	175 mL
1 tbsp	granulated sugar	15 mL

1. Measure all ingredients *except raisins and granulated sugar* into machine's baking pan in the order recommended by the manufacturer. Insert pan into the oven chamber. Select **Dough Cycle**.

2. Stop bread machine when the kneading portion of the cycle is complete. (Do not allow dough to rise in the machine.) Remove dough to a lightly floured surface. Cover with a large bowl and let rest for 10 to 15 minutes. Knead in the raisins. Shape the dough into a round cylinder 13 1/2 inches (36 cm) long. Cut into 9 equal slices, each 1 1/2 inches (4 cm) thick. Push thumbs through the center of each slice and pull into a bagel shape, rounding all surfaces. Place on prepared baking sheet. Cover and let rise in a warm, draft-free place for 15 to 20 minutes. Meanwhile, preheat oven to 400° F (200° C).

3. Bring a large pot of water to a gentle (but full) boil; add sugar. Immerse bagels one at a time in water, turning upside-down. With a skimmer or large spoon, hold bagel under the water for 20 seconds or until dough becomes a little puffy. Place on prepared baking sheet or, if using, preheated baking stone. Bake in preheated oven for 15 to 20 minutes or until bagels sound hollow when tapped on the bottom.

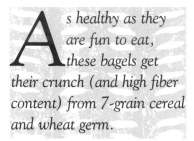

*A*s healthy as they are fun to eat, these bagels get their crunch (and high fiber content) from 7-grain cereal and wheat germ.

Tip

Check the user's manual for your bread machine to get an idea of how long the kneading portion of the **Dough Cycle** will be.

Variation

For a 3-grain version of these bagels, substitute Red River Cereal for the 7-grain variety.

Multigrain Bagels

Makes 9 bagels

Baking sheet, lightly greased
Preheated baking stone (optional)

1 1/4 cups	water	300 mL
1 1/4 tsp	salt	6 mL
2 tbsp	honey	25 mL
1 cup	whole wheat flour	250 mL
2 1/4 cups	bread flour	550 mL
3/4 cup	7-grain cereal	175 mL
1/4 cup	wheat germ	50 mL
2 tsp	bread machine yeast	10 mL
1 tbsp	granulated sugar	15 mL

1. Measure ingredients *except granulated sugar* into baking pan in the order recommended by the manufacturer. Insert pan into the oven chamber. Select **Dough Cycle**.

2. Stop bread machine when the kneading portion of the cycle is complete. (Do not allow dough to rise in the machine.) Remove dough to a lightly floured surface. Cover with a large bowl and let rest for 10 to 15 minutes. Shape the dough into a round cylinder 13 1/2 inches (36 cm) long. Cut into 9 equal slices, each 1 1/2 inches (4 cm) thick. Push thumbs through the center of each slice and pull into a bagel shape, rounding all surfaces. Place on prepared baking sheet. Cover and let rise in a warm, draft-free place for 15 to 20 minutes. Meanwhile, preheat oven to 400° F (200° C).

3. Bring a large pot of water to a gentle (but full) boil; add sugar. Immerse bagels one at a time in water, turning upside-down. With a skimmer or large spoon, hold bagel under the water for 20 seconds or until dough becomes a little puffy. Place on prepared baking sheet or on preheated baking stone. Bake in preheated oven for 15 to 20 minutes or until bagels sound hollow when tapped on the bottom.

NEW BEGINNINGS FOR SOURDOUGHS: STARTERS VS. SOURS

From the time of the early settlers, sourdough breads have required a starter — essentially, a fermented mix of yeast, water, flour and sugar. Traditional starters were maintained for years (often many generations) with periodic "feedings" of sugar, as well as additions of flour and water to replenish any starter used for making sourdough. While the traditional starter method has a certain charm, and makes wonderfully tangy breads and rolls, it is time-consuming and, with variations in temperature and humidity, can produce inconsistent results.

In recent years, a new type of product has been introduced as an alternative to sourdough starters. These are called "dry active sourdough cultures". Sold under brand names such as lalvain du jour® and SAF Levain, these don't require all the time and care that starters do. Simply make up a "sour," then use it for baking. When finished, make a fresh batch of sour from a new package. The results are more consistent.

Purchasing lalvain du jour®
Visit www.lallemand.com or phone 1-877-fermipan

Visit www.KingArthurFlour.com or phone 1-800-827-6836.

Using sours
Prepared BASIC SOUR MIX (see recipe, facing page) should be measured and used directly from the refrigerator.

Stir well before each use. It is normal for a sour to separate. The liquid rises to the top, while a very white, thick part settles to the bottom of the storage container.

A fresh sour is less gassy and therefore bakes a loaf with finer texture.

Storing sour and dry active sourdough cultures
Store prepared sour in refrigerator, covered, for up to 4 weeks. For longer storage, measure the amount called for in the recipe, wrap and over-wrap; freeze for up to 3 months. Thaw in the refrigerator before using. Use cold from the refrigerator.

Store unopened and opened dry active sourdough culture packages in the refrigerator.

*F*or many generations, artisan bakers have used traditional starter to make their sourdough. Today we can duplicate their techniques and results with dry active sourdough culture and a bread machine.

Tip

Sours must be made ahead, allowed to ferment at room temperature, stored, then used as the "starter" in a recipe.

5 lbs (2.5 kg) of flour is equal to about 20 cups (5 L).

This recipe can be halved or quartered. Mix the contents of the dry active sourdough culture package well before measuring.

Basic Sour Mix

28 cups	water (warmed to 98° F [37° C])	7 L
1 tbsp	granulated sugar	15 mL
5 lbs	bread flour	2.5 kg
1	pkg (0.17 oz [5 g]) dry active sourdough culture	1

1. In a large plastic storage container, combine water, sugar, flour and dry active sourdough culture; mix until well blended. Any remaining lumps of flour will disappear as the sour develops. Cover tightly and let stand in a warm, draft-free place for 18 to 24 hours. Refrigerate overnight before using.

TIPS FOR WORKING WITH SOURDOUGH

Sourdough loaves have a crisper crust, a more open interior and a "tuggier" texture than traditional loaves.

The method of preparing and baking sourdough is also quite different from that used for conventional breads. Here are some hints to make sour-dough baking more rewarding.

1. Preparing

Although traditional artisan breads do not contain sugar or fat, adding a small amount of sugar may result in a more open texture. The dough should be sticky. Resist the temptation to add more flour, since this will make the loaf tougher.

2. Resting

Place dough on the generous-ly floured lid of a large plastic storage container. Dust the top of the dough with flour, cover with the container and tightly seal. Let the dough rest, at room temperature, for 45 min-utes to 1 hour before forming. Do not grease the storage container or the dough.

3. Forming

On a floured surface, flatten the dough into a rectangle with the heel of your hand. Fold one-third of the dough over. With the heel of your hand, seal the seam. Repeat with the remaining third from the opposite side. Seal the seam. Rotate the dough by one-quarter turn. Roll into a log shape, sealing the seam well. Place the formed dough, seam-side down, on the gen-erously floured lid of a large plastic storage container. Dust the top of the dough with rice flour, cover with the container and tightly seal. (Rice flour stays white during baking — unlike wheat flour, which browns.)

4. Proofing

Proof dough in the refrigerator for at least 14 hours. This slow, cool-rise produces the bread's open texture.

5. Slashing

Slash the risen dough with a *lame* or a sharp knife. (For instructions on this procedure, see Techniques Glossary, page 184.) For long, narrow loaves, make 3 to 5 diagonal slashes; round-shaped loaves can be slashed with an "X" pattern. Dust again with rice flour before baking.

6. Baking

Remove the dough from the refrigerator 30 minutes before baking. Slide the risen dough onto a baking sheet, a baguette pan or a preheated baking stone. Bake in pre-heated oven.

For a crispy crust, steam the dough immediately after putting it in the oven. See Techniques Glossary, page 183, for instructions on the procedure.

Tempt your palate with the flavor of this tangy sourdough, with its combination of raisins, rye and walnuts.

Tip

See "Tips for Working with Sourdough," on facing page.

See Techniques Glossary, page 183, for instructions on injecting steam.

French Walnut Raisin Sourdough

Makes 2 loaves

Large plastic storage container, lid generously floured

Baking sheet, sprinkled with cornmeal *or* preheated baking stone

1 1/2 cups	cold BASIC SOUR MIX (see recipe, page 89)	375 mL
1 1/4 tsp	salt	6 mL
2/3 cup	whole-wheat bread flour	150 mL
1 1/3 cups	bread flour	325 mL
1/3 cup	rye flour	75 mL
3/4 cup	chopped walnuts	175 mL
1/2 cup	raisins	125 mL
1 tbsp	bread machine yeast	15 mL

1. Measure ingredients into baking pan in the order recommended by the manufacturer. Insert baking pan into oven chamber. Select **Dough Cycle**.

2. Stop bread machine when the kneading portion of the cycle is complete. (Do not allow dough to rise in the machine.) Place the dough on prepared storage container lid. Lightly flour the dough. Cover and tightly seal with inverted storage container base. Let rise for 45 minutes to 1 hour in a warm, draft-free place.

3. Divide risen dough in half. Form each half into a round loaf. Place each on the re-floured lid. Cover tightly and refrigerate for at least 14 hours or overnight.

4. Remove the dough from the refrigerator 30 minutes before baking. Preheat oven to 400° F (200° C). Place loaves on prepared baking sheets or preheated baking stone. (For crispier crust, steam dough using technique described on page 184). Bake in preheated oven for 10 minutes. Reduce the oven temperature to 350° F (180° C) and bake for 15 to 20 minutes or until loaves sound hollow when tapped on the bottom.

These aren't your average hamburger buns! The flavor trio of cheese, onion and sourdough is sensational.

Tip

Sourdough will be sticky. Flour your fingers for easier handling.

Variation

This recipe can also be used to make 4 submarine buns.

Onion Cheddar Sourdough Hamburger Buns

Makes 8 buns

Large plastic storage container, lid generously floured

Baking sheet, dusted with cornmeal

1 3/4 cups	cold BASIC SOUR MIX (see recipe, page 89)	425 mL
1 tsp	salt	5 mL
3 1/4 cups	bread flour	800 mL
3/4 cup	grated aged Cheddar cheese	175 mL
2 tbsp	minced dry onion	25 mL
1 3/4 tsp	bread machine yeast	8 mL

1. Measure ingredients into baking pan in the order recommended by the manufacturer. Insert pan into the oven chamber. Select **Dough Cycle**.

2. Stop bread machine when the kneading portion of the cycle is complete. (Do not allow dough to rise in the machine.) Place the dough on prepared storage container lid. Lightly flour the dough. Cover and tightly seal with inverted storage container base. Let rise for 45 minutes to 1 hour in a warm, draft-free place.

3. Divide dough into 8 portions. Form each into a hamburger bun, flattening tops slightly. Place on re-floured lid and cover tightly. Refrigerate for at least 14 hours or overnight.

4. Remove the dough from the refrigerator 30 minutes before baking. Preheat oven to 375° F (190° C). Place buns on prepared baking sheet. Bake in preheated oven for 25 to 35 minutes or until buns sound hollow when tapped on the bottom.

*S*pread baguettes with Brie cheese or chèvre and top with roasted vegetables for a delicious light lunch.

Tip

For information about baguette pans, see Equipment Glossary, page 176.

Variation

Use the dough to make 1 large loaf.

Sourdough Baguettes

Makes 2 baguettes

Large plastic storage container, lid generously floured

Baguette pan or baking sheet, sprinkled with cornmeal

1 3/4 cups	cold BASIC SOUR MIX (see recipe, page 89)	425 mL
1 1/2 tsp	salt	7 mL
1 tsp	granulated sugar	5 mL
3 3/4 cups	bread flour	925 mL
1 1/2 tsp	bread machine yeast	7 mL

1. Measure ingredients into baking pan in the order recommended by the manufacturer. Insert pan into the oven chamber. Select **Dough Cycle**.

2. Stop bread machine when the kneading portion of the cycle is complete. (Do not allow dough to rise in the machine.) Place the dough on prepared storage container lid. Lightly flour top of dough. Cover and tightly seal with inverted storage container base. Let rise for 45 minutes to 1 hour in a warm, draft-free place.

3. Divide dough in half. Form each half into a thin stick 14 inches (35 cm) long, tapering at both ends. Place both on the re-floured lid and dust with flour. Cover tightly and refrigerate for at least 14 hours or overnight.

4. Remove the dough from the refrigerator 30 minutes before baking. Preheat oven to 450° F (220° C). Place the dough on prepared baguette pan or baking sheet. (For crispier crust, steam dough using technique described on page 184). Bake in preheated oven for 10 minutes. Reduce oven temperature to 400° F (200° C) and bake for 8 to 10 minutes if using a baguette pan and 15 to 20 minutes if using a baking sheet, until baguettes sound hollow when tapped on the bottom.

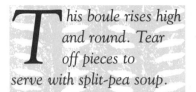

*T*his boule rises high and round. Tear off pieces to serve with split-pea soup.

Tip

For instructions on steaming, see Techniques Glossary (page 184).

For a professional finish, use a *banneton* (see Equipment Glossary, page 176) or a generously floured wicker basket that is twice the size of the unrisen dough. Place dough in basket, then in large plastic container; cover tightly and refrigerate as in step 3. Gently tip it out of the basket upside down onto a prepared baking sheet. Bake as directed in step 4.

Sourdough Boule

Makes 1 boule

Large plastic storage container, lid generously floured

Banneton, optional (see note at left)

Baking sheet, sprinkled with cornmeal

1 1/3 cups	cold BASIC SOUR MIX (see recipe, page 89)	325 mL
1 1/4 tsp	salt	6 mL
1 tbsp	honey	15 mL
2 1/4 cups	bread flour	550 mL
1/2 cup	rye flour	125 mL
2 tsp	bread machine yeast	10 mL

1. Measure ingredients into baking pan in the order recommended by the manufacturer. Insert pan into the oven chamber. Select **Dough Cycle**.

2. Stop bread machine when the kneading portion of the cycle is complete. (Do not allow dough to rise in the machine.) Remove dough to a lightly floured surface. Cover with a large bowl and let rest for 10 to 15 minutes. Place the dough on prepared storage container lid. Lightly flour top of dough and cover and tightly seal with inverted storage container base. Let rise for 45 minutes to 1 hour in a warm, draft-free place.

3. Form into a high rounded ball. Place dough on the re-floured lid and dust with flour (or in *banneton*, if using) and seal in a storage container. Cover tightly and refrigerate for at least 14 hours or overnight.

4. Remove the dough from the refrigerator 30 minutes before baking. Preheat oven to 400° F (200° C). Place the dough on prepared baking sheet. Inject steam (see page 183). Bake in preheated oven for 10 minutes. Reduce oven temperature to 350° F (180° C) and bake for 20 to 25 minutes or until boule sounds hollow when tapped on the bottom.

Sweet Doughs and Loaves

Tips for making sweet yeast breads   96

Whole Wheat Applesauce Loaf   97

Almond-Filled Christmas Cranberry Kringle   98

Autumn Pumpkin Loaf   100

Blueberry Peach Streusel Cake   102

Blueberry Poppy Loaf   104

Daffodil Bread   105

Date Orange Bundles   106

Cranberry Raisin Loaf   108

Hawaiian Sunrise Bread   109

Hazelnut Chocolate Bread   110

Nanaimo Bar Loaf   111

Orange Glazed Breakfast Cake   112

Ranging from the lightly sweet to the super-saccharin, these loaves are delicious served warm from the oven as a snack or dessert.

TIPS FOR MAKING SWEET YEAST BREADS

When adding fruit and/or nuts at the "add ingredients" signal, scrape any dry ingredients out of the corners of the baking pan with a rubber spatula.

Very sweet or rich dough requires more proofing time than standard breads. Be patient! It may take over an hour.

After baking, remove the loaf immediately from the bread machine or oven and transfer to a wire cooling rack. If set on a plate, the bottom of the loaf will become soggy.

For maximum freshness, wrap sweet loaves airtight and store at room temperature. (They'll become stale more quickly in the refrigerator.) Watch for the development of mold during hot, humid weather.

While they shouldn't be refrigerated, sweet yeast breads and coffee cakes freeze well. Allow to cool completely before wrapping airtight for the freezer. It's best to over-wrap the bread. Freeze up to 6 weeks. When ready to use, thaw the bread, being sure to keep it wrapped so that it doesn't dry out.

For a fresher, more attractive appearance, glaze the loaf, then decorate it with toasted nuts and fruit wedges.

TUSCAN WALNUT TOASTIES (PAGE 66) ➤

OVERLEAF (FROM LOWER LEFT): SUN-DRIED TOMATO LAVOSH (PAGE 52);
SOURDOUGH BAGUETTES (PAGE 93)

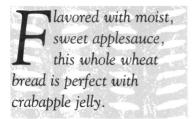

*F*lavored with moist, sweet applesauce, this whole wheat bread is perfect with crabapple jelly.

Tip

If your bread machine does not have an "add ingredient" signal on the **Whole Wheat Cycle**, add the raisins on top of the flour — or check the manufacturers' directions for use — then set a timer for 5 minutes before the end of the second long knead.

Variation

Substitute cinnamon for the ginger.

Whole Wheat Applesauce Loaf

1.5 LB (750 G)

1 1/4 cups	unsweetened applesauce (room temperature)	300 mL
1	egg	1
1 1/2 tsp	salt	7 mL
2 tbsp	packed brown sugar	25 mL
1 tbsp	molasses	15 mL
2 tbsp	vegetable oil	25 mL
2 cups	whole-wheat flour	500 mL
1 cup	bread flour	250 mL
1 tsp	ground ginger	5 mL
1 1/2 tsp	bread machine yeast	7 mL
2/3 cup	raisins	150 mL

2 LB (1 KG)

1 1/2 cups	unsweetened applesauce (room temperature)	375 mL
1	egg	1
1 1/2 tsp	salt	7 mL
3 tbsp	packed brown sugar	45 mL
1 tbsp	molasses	15 mL
2 tbsp	vegetable oil	25 mL
2 cups	whole-wheat flour	500 mL
1 1/2 cups	bread flour	375 mL
1 1/2 tsp	ground ginger	7 mL
2 tsp	bread machine yeast	10 mL
3/4 cup	raisins	175 mL

1. Measure all ingredients *except raisins* into baking pan in the order recommended by the manufacturer. Insert pan into the oven chamber. Select **Whole Wheat Cycle**. Add raisins at "add ingredient" signal. (See Tip, at left, if your machine does not have this signal on the whole wheat cycle.)

‹ MAPLE BANANA FLAXSEED BREAD (PAGE 78)

*F*or an elegant Christmas brunch, place the Kringle on the center of the table. Garnish with holly and fresh cranberries. Serve with clementines and a tray of assorted cheeses.

Tip

To soften almond paste that has dried, place in an airtight plastic bag with a slice of bread. As it softens, break off pieces to allow moisture to soften the remaining block.

Almond Filled Christmas Cranberry Kringle

Makes 1 Kringle

Baking sheet, lightly greased

Bread

1 cup	milk (room temperature)	250 mL
1	egg	1
1 1/4 tsp	salt	6 mL
3 tbsp	granulated sugar	45 mL
1/4 cup	butter	50 mL
3 3/4 cups	bread flour	925 mL
1/2 cup	fresh cranberries	125 mL
1/2 tsp	ground cardamom	2 mL
1/2 tsp	cinnamon	2 mL
1 1/2 tsp	bread machine yeast	7 mL

Almond Filling

1/4 cup	softened butter	50 mL
1/4 cup	almond paste	50 mL
3 tbsp	all-purpose flour	45 mL
1 1/2 tsp	lemon zest	7 mL
1/4 cup	packed brown sugar	50 mL
1	egg white	1
1 tsp	vanilla	5 mL
3/4 tsp	ground cardamom	4 mL
3/4 cup	fresh cranberries	175 mL
1/2 cup	chopped pecans	125 mL

Egg Yolk Glaze

1	egg yolk	1
2 tbsp	water	25 mL

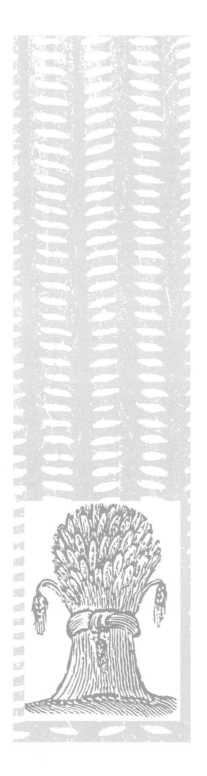

1. Measure bread ingredients into machine's baking pan in the order recommended by the manufacturer. Insert pan into the oven chamber. Select **Dough Cycle**.

2. Filling: In a large bowl, beat together butter and almond paste until creamy. Add flour, zest, brown sugar, egg white, vanilla and cardamom; whip until smooth and set aside.

3. Remove dough to a lightly floured surface. Cover with a large bowl and let rest for 10 to 15 minutes. Roll out the dough to a 15- by 10-inch (37.5 by 25 cm) rectangle. Spread with filling. Sprinkle with cranberries and pecans. Beginning at the long side, roll jellyroll-style. Pinch to seal seam. Form into a wreath, pinching ends to seal. Place on prepared baking sheet, seam-side down. Cover and let rise in a warm, draft-free place for 30 to 45 minutes or until doubled in volume. Meanwhile, preheat oven to 375° F (190° C).

4. Glaze: In a small bowl, whisk together egg yolk and water. Brush the risen dough with glaze. Cut 4 slits in the wreath. Bake in preheated oven for 30 to 35 minutes or until wreath sounds hollow when tapped on the bottom. Serve warm from the oven or cooled to room temperature.

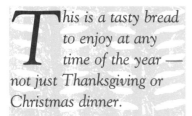

*T*his is a tasty bread to enjoy at any time of the year — not just Thanksgiving or Christmas dinner.

Tip

Be sure to buy pumpkin purée — not pumpkin pie filling, which is too sweet and contains too much moisture for this recipe.

Yes, you're reading it right: The 1.5 lb (750 g) recipe contains *more* yeast than the 2 lb (1 kg).

Variation

Substitute butterscotch chips for the dried cranberries. Add them with the other ingredients; there's no need to wait for the "add ingredient" signal.

Autumn Pumpkin Loaf

Makes 1 loaf

1.5 LB (750 G)

1/2 cup	water	125 mL
1/2 cup	canned pumpkin purée	125 mL
1	egg	1
1/4 cup	nonfat dry milk	50 mL
1 1/4 tsp	salt	6 mL
1/4 cup	granulated sugar	50 mL
2 tbsp	shortening	25 mL
2 3/4 cups	bread flour	725 mL
1/2 tsp	ground allspice	2 mL
1/4 tsp	ground ginger	1 mL
1/4 tsp	ground nutmeg	1 mL
1 1/4 tsp	bread machine yeast	6 mL
1/4 cup	dried cranberries	50 mL
1/4 cup	pumpkin seeds	50 mL

2 LB (1 KG)

2/3 cup	water	150 mL
2/3 cup	canned pumpkin purée	150 mL
2	eggs	2
1/3 cup	nonfat dry milk	75 mL
1 1/2 tsp	salt	7 mL
1/4 cup	granulated sugar	50 mL
2 tbsp	shortening	25 mL
3 1/2 cups	bread flour	875 mL
1/2 tsp	ground allspice	2 mL
1/4 tsp	ground ginger	1 mL
1/4 tsp	ground nutmeg	1 mL
1 tsp	bread machine yeast	5 mL
1/3 cup	dried cranberries	75 mL
1/3 cup	pumpkin seeds	75 mL

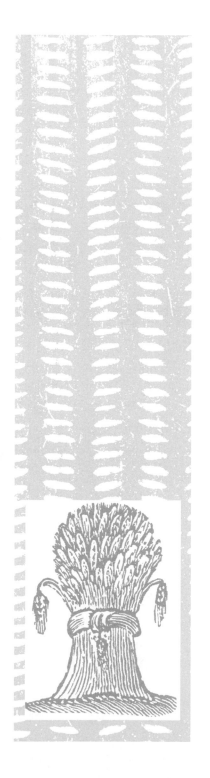

1. Measure all ingredients *except dried cranberries and pumpkin seeds* into baking pan in the order recommended by the manufacturer. Insert pan into the oven chamber. Select **Sweet Cycle**. Add dried cranberries and pumpkin seeds at "add ingredient" signal.

*P*repare this streusel cake when the farmers' markets are overflowing with ripe, luscious (and inexpensive) summer fruit.

Tip

Unwashed blueberries can be frozen for up to 2 months without losing flavor or quality. When ready to use, rinse frozen berries quickly under cold water and dry well. No need to thaw.

Variation

Substitute 4 cups (1 L) of sliced apples (or another seasonal fruit) for the peaches. Place in overlapping circles for an attractive design.

Blueberry Peach Streusel Cake

Makes 2 cakes

Two 10-inch (3 L) springform pans, bottoms lightly greased

Cake

1/2 cup	water	125 mL
1/2 cup	orange juice	125 mL
2 tsp	orange zest	10 mL
1/4 cup	nonfat dry milk	50 mL
1	egg	1
1 1/2 tsp	salt	7 mL
1/4 cup	packed brown sugar	50 mL
2 tbsp	butter	25 mL
3 1/4 cups	bread flour	800 mL
1/2 tsp	ground nutmeg	2 mL
1 1/2 tsp	bread machine yeast	7 mL

Fruit Filling

4 cups	sliced fresh peaches	1 L
2 cups	fresh blueberries	500 mL

Streusel Topping

2 cups	packed brown sugar	500 mL
1/2 cup	all-purpose flour	125 mL
4 tsp	orange zest	20 mL
6 tbsp	butter, melted	90 mL
2 cups	sliced almonds	500 mL

1. Cake: Measure ingredients into machine's baking pan in the order recommended by the manufacturer. Insert pan into the oven chamber. Select **Dough Cycle**.

2. Filling: In a large bowl, combine peaches and blueberries; set aside.

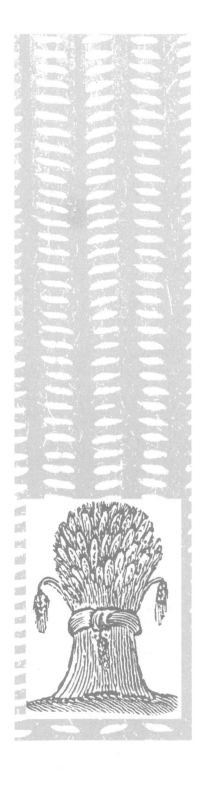

3. Topping: In a small bowl, combine brown sugar, flour and orange zest. Add melted butter and mix until crumbly; set aside.

4. Remove dough to a lightly floured surface. Cover with a large bowl and let rest for 10 to 15 minutes. Divide dough in half. Press one portion of the dough into one prepared pan. Top with half of the prepared filling. Sprinkle with half of the topping and then half of the sliced almonds. Repeat with the second pan. Cover and let rise in a warm, draft-free place for 45 to 60 minutes or until doubled in volume. Meanwhile, preheat oven to 350° F (180° C).

5. Bake in preheated oven for 40 to 45 minutes or until streusel cake is golden brown. Serve warm from the oven or at room temperature.

*T*his light-textured loaf is one of our friend Patti's favorites. She loves the unique flavor and richness it gets from the sour cream.

Tip

This is an extra-large loaf. To avoid the top of the loaf hitting the lid of the bread machine, try the 1.5 lb (750 g) loaf first.

Yes, you're reading it right: The 1.5 lb (750 g) recipe contains *more* yeast than the 2 lb (1 kg).

Variation

Dried currants can be substituted for the blueberries and orange zest for the lemon.

Blueberry Poppy Loaf

1.5 LB (750 G)

1 1/2 cups	sour cream	375 mL
1 tsp	lemon zest	5 mL
1 tsp	salt	5 mL
2 tbsp	granulated sugar	25 mL
1 tbsp	vegetable oil	15 mL
2 3/4 cups	bread flour	675 mL
1/3 cup	poppy seeds	75 mL
1 1/2 tsp	bread machine yeast	6 mL
1/3 cup	dried blueberries	75 mL

2 LB (1 KG)   L

2 cups	sour cream	500 mL
2 tsp	lemon zest	10 mL
1 1/2 tsp	salt	7 mL
3 tbsp	granulated sugar	45 mL
2 tbsp	vegetable oil	25 mL
4 cups	bread flour	1000 mL
1/2 cup	poppy seeds	125 mL
1 tsp	bread machine yeast	5 mL
1/2 cup	dried blueberries	125 mL

1. Measure all ingredients *except dried blueberries* into baking pan in the order recommended by the manufacturer. Insert pan into the oven chamber. Select **Sweet Cycle**. Add dried blueberries at "add ingredient" signal.

*B*ring a little bit of springtime to your table! Enjoy this bread's light texture, combined with the refreshing aroma and flavor of citrus.

Tip

Use a zester for long thin strips of citrus peel. Be sure to remove only the outer skin, avoiding the bitter white pith underneath.

Yes, you're reading it right: The 1.5 lb (750 g) recipe contains the *same* amount of yeast as the 2 lb (1 kg).

Variation

Make this into a lemon bread by using all lemon juice and lemon zest or an orange bread with all orange ingredients.

Daffodil Bread

1.5 LB (750 G)

3/4 cup	water	175 mL
2 tbsp	fresh orange juice	25 mL
1 tbsp	fresh lemon juice	15 mL
1 tbsp	lemon zest	15 mL
1 tbsp	orange zest	15 mL
2	eggs	2
1/4 cup	nonfat dry milk	50 mL
1 1/2 tsp	salt	7 mL
2 tbsp	granulated sugar	25 mL
2 tbsp	butter	25 mL
3 cups	bread flour	750 mL
3/4 tsp	bread machine yeast	3 mL

2 LB (1 KG)   L

1 cup	water	250 mL
2 tbsp	fresh orange juice	25 mL
1 tbsp	fresh lemon juice	15 mL
1 tbsp	lemon zest	15 mL
1 tbsp	orange zest	15 mL
2	eggs	2
1/3 cup	nonfat dry milk	75 mL
1 3/4 tsp	salt	8 mL
3 tbsp	granulated sugar	45 mL
3 tbsp	butter	45 mL
4 cups	bread flour	1000 mL
3/4 tsp	bread machine yeast	3 mL

1. Measure ingredients into baking pan in the order recommended by the manufacturer. Insert pan into the oven chamber. Select **Basic Cycle**.

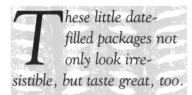

These little date-filled packages not only look irresistible, but taste great, too.

Tip

For best appearance, roll circles thinner at the edges than in the center.

A 12-oz (375 g) package yields about 2 cups (500 mL) dates.

Variation

To complete the presentation, tie a licorice ribbon at the point where dough is pinched near the top.

Try adding 1/4 cup (50 mL) raisins to the dates in the filling.

Date Orange Bundles

Makes 16 bundles

Baking sheet, lightly greased

Bundles

1 cup	milk (room temperature)	250 mL
2 tbsp	thawed frozen orange juice concentrate	25 mL
1 tbsp	orange zest	15 mL
1/4 tsp	orange extract	1 mL
1	egg	1
1 1/4 tsp	salt	6 mL
2 tbsp	granulated sugar	25 mL
1/4 cup	butter	50 mL
3 3/4 cups	bread flour	925 mL
1 tsp	bread machine yeast	5 mL

Date Filling

2 cups	pitted dates	500 mL
1 1/2 cups	water	375 mL

Egg White Glaze

1	egg white	1
1 tbsp	water	15 mL

1. Bundles: Measure ingredients into machine's baking pan in the order recommended by the manufacturer. Insert pan into the oven chamber. Select **Dough Cycle**.

2. Filling: In a saucepan over low heat, combine pitted dates and water. Cook, stirring occasionally, until the dates are soft and have the consistency of jam. Set aside to cool.

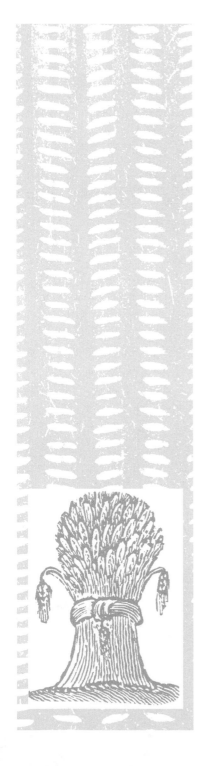

3. Remove dough to a lightly floured surface. Cover with a large bowl and let rest for 10 to 15 minutes. Divide dough into 16 portions. Roll into balls; stretch each into a 5-inch (12.5 cm) circle. Place 2 tbsp (25 mL) filling in the center of each circle. Pull the dough up around the filling, pleating tightly above filling, pinching tightly to seal. Place on prepared baking sheet. Cover and let rise in a warm, draft-free place for 30 to 45 minutes or until doubled in volume. Meanwhile, preheat oven to 350° F (180° C).

4. Glaze: In a small bowl, whisk together egg white and water. Pinch the pleats again in the risen dough and brush with glaze. Bake in preheated oven for 20 to 25 minutes or until bundles sound hollow when tapped on the bottom.

*T*his recipe was inspired by the request of a newsletter subscriber for a raisin bread that is not too sweet.

Tip

The 2 lb (1 kg) loaf may hit the lid of some bread machines. To avoid this, try the 1.5 lb (750 g) recipe first.

Yes, you're reading it right: The 1.5 lb (750 g) recipe contains the *same* amount of yeast as the 2 lb (1 kg).

Variation

Try adding chocolate chips for half the raisins.

Cranberry Raisin Loaf

1.5 LB (750 G)

1 cup	water	250 mL
1	egg	1
1/4 cup	nonfat dry milk	50 mL
1 tsp	salt	5 mL
1 tbsp	packed brown sugar	15 mL
2 tbsp	shortening	25 mL
3 1/4 cups	bread flour	800 mL
1 1/2 tsp	ground cardamom	7 mL
1 tsp	bread machine yeast	4 mL
1/3 cup	dried cranberries	75 mL
1/3 cup	raisins	75 mL

2 LB (1 KG)　　　　　　　　　　　　L

1 1/4 cups	water	375 mL
1	egg	1
1/3 cup	nonfat dry milk	75 mL
1 1/4 tsp	salt	6 mL
2 tbsp	packed brown sugar	25 mL
2 tbsp	shortening	25 mL
3 3/4 cups	bread flour	925 mL
2 tsp	ground cardamom	10 mL
1 tsp	bread machine yeast	4 mL
1/2 cup	dried cranberries	125 mL
1/2 cup	raisins	125 mL

1. Measure all ingredients *except dried cranberries and raisins* into baking pan in the order recommended by the manufacturer. Insert pan into the oven chamber. Select **Sweet Cycle**. Add dried cranberries and raisins at "add ingredient" signal.

*B*ring the fragrance and flavor of the Hawaiian islands to your table with this light, angel food-like loaf.

Tip

In this recipe you can add the fruit and nuts directly with the other ingredients — no need to wait for the "add ingredient" signal.

For instructions on toasting coconut, see Techniques Glossary, page 183.

Yes, you're reading it right: The 1.5 lb (750 g) recipe contains *more* yeast than the 2 lb (1 kg).

Variation

To add multi-colored flecks to the loaf, try adding "confetti-style" coconut.

Hawaiian Sunrise Bread

1.5 LB (750 G)

1 1/4 cups	water	300 mL
1/4 cup	nonfat dry milk	50 mL
1 tsp	salt	5 mL
1 tbsp	granulated sugar	15 mL
1 tbsp	shortening	15 mL
3 cups	bread flour	750 mL
1/3 cup	shredded toasted unsweetened coconut	75 mL
1/3 cup	glazed pineapple chunks	75 mL
1/4 cup	coarsely chopped Macadamia nuts	50 mL
1 tsp	bread machine yeast	5 mL

2 LB (1 KG)

1 1/2 cups	water	375 mL
1/3 cup	nonfat dry milk	75 mL
1 1/4 tsp	salt	6 mL
1 tbsp	granulated sugar	15 mL
1 tbsp	shortening	15 mL
4 cups	bread flour	1000 mL
1/2 cup	shredded toasted unsweetened coconut	125 mL
1/2 cup	glazed pineapple chunks	125 mL
1/3 cup	coarsely chopped Macadamia nuts	75 mL
3/4 tsp	bread machine yeast	4 mL

1. Measure ingredients into baking pan in the order recommended by the manufacturer. Insert pan into the oven chamber. Select **Sweet Cycle**.

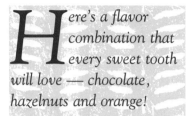

ere's a flavor combination that every sweet tooth will love — chocolate, hazelnuts and orange!

Tip

For instructions on removing hazelnut skins, see Techniques Glossary, page 183.

Melt the chocolate in the microwave just until soft.

Yes, you're reading it right: The 1.5 lb (750 g) recipe contains the *same* amount of yeast as the 2 lb (1 kg).

Variation

Substitute a cherry-flavored liqueur, such as Cherry Heering, for the hazelnut liqueur.

Replace the hazelnut liqueur with additional orange juice concentrate.

Hazelnut Chocolate Bread

1.5 LB (750 G)

1 cup	water	250 mL
2 tbsp	thawed frozen orange juice concentrate	25 mL
1 tbsp	hazelnut liqueur	15 mL
2 tsp	orange zest	10 mL
1 oz	unsweetened chocolate, melted	30 g
1 tsp	salt	5 mL
1/4 cup	granulated sugar	50 mL
1 tbsp	butter	15 mL
3 cups	bread flour	750 mL
1/4 cup	chopped hazelnuts	50 mL
3 tbsp	unsweetened cocoa	45 mL
1 1/2 tsp	bread machine yeast	7 mL

2 LB (1 KG)

1 1/4 cups	water	300 mL
2 tbsp	thawed frozen orange juice concentrate	25 mL
2 tbsp	hazelnut liqueur	25 mL
1 tbsp	orange zest	15 mL
1 oz	unsweetened chocolate, melted	30 g
1 1/4 tsp	salt	6 mL
1/3 cup	granulated sugar	75 mL
1 tbsp	butter	15 mL
3 1/2 cups	bread flour	875 mL
1/3 cup	chopped hazelnuts	75 mL
1/4 cup	unsweetened cocoa	50 mL
1 1/2 tsp	bread machine yeast	7 mL

1. Measure ingredients into baking pan in the order recommended by the manufacturer. Insert pan into the oven chamber. Select **Sweet Cycle**.

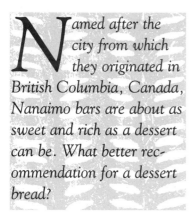

amed after the city from which they originated in British Columbia, Canada, Nanaimo bars are about as sweet and rich as a dessert can be. What better recommendation for a dessert bread?

Tip

Some bread machines bake hotter than others. These may partially melt the chocolate chips in this recipe, giving the loaf a marbled look.

Yes, you're reading it right: The 1.5 lb (750 g) recipe contains *more* yeast than the 2 lb (1 kg).

Variation

Substitute white chocolate, butterscotch or peanut butter chips for the chocolate chips.

Nanaimo Bar Loaf

1.5 LB (750 G)

1 cup	water	250 mL
1 tsp	salt	5 mL
3 tbsp	granulated sugar	45 mL
2 tbsp	shortening	25 mL
3 1/4 cups	bread flour	800 mL
1 tbsp	unsweetened cocoa	15 mL
1/2 cup	unsweetened flaked coconut	125 mL
1/2 cup	chopped pecans	125 mL
1/3 cup	chocolate chips	75 mL
1 1/2 tsp	bread machine yeast	7 mL

2 LB (1 KG)

1 1/4 cups	water	300 mL
1 1/4 tsp	salt	6 mL
1/4 cup	granulated sugar	50 mL
2 tbsp	shortening	25 mL
4 cups	bread flour	1000 mL
1 tbsp	unsweetened cocoa	15 mL
2/3 cup	unsweetened flaked coconut	150 mL
2/3 cup	chopped pecans	150 mL
1/2 cup	chocolate chips	125 mL
1 1/4 tsp	bread machine yeast	6 mL

1. Measure ingredients into baking pan in the order recommended by the manufacturer. Insert pan into the oven chamber. Select **Sweet Cycle**.

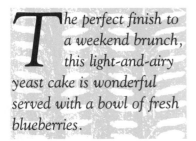

The perfect finish to a weekend brunch, this light-and-airy yeast cake is wonderful served with a bowl of fresh blueberries.

Tip

Any type of cottage cheese — large or small curd, high- or low-fat — will work well in this recipe.

Variation

Substitute lemon juice for the orange juice in the glaze.

Orange Glazed Breakfast Cake

Makes 1 cake

Tube pan, lightly greased

Cake

1/2 cup	water	125 mL
1/2 cup	fresh orange juice	125 mL
1/2 cup	cottage cheese	125 mL
1	egg	1
2 tsp	orange zest	10 mL
3/4 tsp	salt	4 mL
2 tbsp	granulated sugar	25 mL
2 tbsp	butter	25 mL
4 cups	bread flour	1000 mL
1 1/2 tsp	bread machine yeast	7 mL

Orange Glaze

1 cup	sifted confectioner's sugar	250 mL
1 to 2 tbsp	fresh orange juice	15 to 25 mL

1. Measure the cake ingredients into machine's baking pan in the order recommended by the manufacturer. Insert pan into the oven chamber. Select **Dough Cycle**.

2. Remove dough to a lightly floured surface. Cover with a large bowl and let rest for 10 to 15 minutes. Divide the dough into 3 portions. Roll each into an 18-inch (45 cm) rope. Braid the three ropes. Place in prepared tube pan, pinching ends together to form a ring. Cover and let rise in a warm, draft-free place for 30 to 45 minutes or until doubled in volume. Preheat oven to 350° F (180° C).

3. Bake in preheated oven for 30 to 35 minutes or until the breakfast cake sounds hollow when tapped on the bottom. In a bowl, combine confectioner's sugar and orange juice; mix until smooth. Drizzle over the warm breakfast cake.

INTERNATIONAL BREADS

Keeping traditions	114
Irish Barm Bran Bread	115
Baba au Rhum	116
Baltic Birthday Bread	118
Cranberry Walnut Kaffeekuchen	120
Irish Freckle Bread	122
Kolaches	123
Mediterranean Bread	124
Radar Kuchen	125
Ukrainian Egg Bread (Kolach)	126
Swiss Rye Loaf	128

Bread-making traditions from other countries provide a wide range of tastes and textures for us to enjoy. Try these recipes — and explore the world!

KEEPING TRADITIONS

The heritage of each nationality is reflected in its food. And we, as a nation of immigrants, have benefitted from all the different styles of baking that have been brought to these shores. Over the years, these Old World breads and loaves have been adapted to North American ingredients and tastes. Here, we retain the original flavors and textures, adapting the recipes further for the bread machine.

From Ireland we get the unique flavors of raisin and caraway in IRISH FRECKLE BREAD (page 122) and the hearty goodnes of IRISH BARM BRAN BREAD (page 115).

In Germany the earliest sweeteners were honey and dried fruits — a tradition that is carried on in baking holiday breads today.

The Ukrainians celebrate the holidays by serving a KOLACH (page 126), which translates as "circle." It is shaped into a three-tiered circle to symbolize the Trinity.

In addition to the recipes in this chapter, other international breads — including flatbreads such as pitas, cibatta and focaccia, as well as MOROCCAN ANISE BREAD — can be found in Chapter 3, (pages 41 to 56). Be sure to try them all!

*T*his hearty barm (Gaelic for "yeast") bread was the perfect choice for a St. Patrick's Day dinner we hosted. With 176 guests, we needed (or kneaded!) 48 hearth breads — requiring the services of just about every bread machine in our test kitchen to prepare the dough.

Tip

To get the quantity exactly right, add the amount of water called for to a 2-cup (500 mL) glass measure. Then add the yogurt until the level reaches the correct total volume of both ingredients.

For instructions on cooking wheat berries, see Techniques Glossary (page 183).

Variation

Try making rolls with this recipe: Just divide the dough into 12 to 16 equal portions then finish as directed.

Irish Barm Bran Bread

Makes 2 loaves

Baking sheet, lightly greased

Bread

1 cup	water	250 mL
1/2 cup	plain yogurt	125 mL
1 1/2 tsp	salt	7 mL
3 tbsp	honey	45 mL
2 tbsp	shortening	25 mL
1 1/2 cups	whole-wheat flour	375 mL
1 1/2 cups	bread flour	375 mL
1/2 cup	cooked wheat berries	125 mL
1 /2 cup	quick-cooking oats	125 mL
1/2 cup	wheat bran	125 mL
1 1/2 tsp	bread machine yeast	7 mL

Oatmeal Finish

1	egg yolk	1
1 tbsp	water	15 mL
1/4 cup	large-flake oats	50 mL

1. Measure bread ingredients into machine's baking pan in the order recommended by the manufacturer. Insert pan into the oven chamber. Select **Dough Cycle**.

2. Remove dough to a lightly floured surface. Cover with a large bowl and let rest for 10 to 15 minutes. Divide dough in half. Form each into a 6-inch (15 cm) round with a slightly flattened top. Place on prepared baking sheet. Cover and let rise in a warm, draft-free place for 30 to 45 minutes or until doubled in volume. Meanwhile, preheat oven to 350° F (180° C).

3. When dough has risen, using a pizza wheel or a sharp knife, score tops with 8 equally spaced cuts 1/2 inch (1 cm) deep. In a small bowl, whisk together egg yolk and water until smooth; brush over dough and sprinkle with oats. Bake in preheated oven for 35 to 40 minutes or until hearth breads sound hollow when tapped on the bottom.

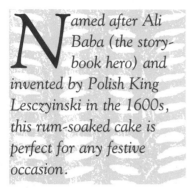

*N*amed after Ali Baba (the story-book hero) and invented by Polish King Lesczyinski in the 1600s, this rum-soaked cake is perfect for any festive occasion.

Tip

More like a stiff batter, this dough will be too sticky to handle; resist the urge to add flour.

The rum syrup can also be prepared in the microwave.

Variation

For a "Baba au Orange," replace rum with additional orange juice. Melt orange marmalade and brush over top of the cake.

Baba au Rhum

Makes 1 cake

Bundt or tube pan, well-greased and floured

Cake

1 1/4 cups	milk (room temperature)	300 mL
2	eggs	2
1 1/2 tsp	salt	7 mL
3 tbsp	granulated sugar	45 mL
2 tbsp	butter	25 mL
3 1/4 cups	bread flour	800 mL
1 1/2 tsp	bread machine yeast	7 mL

Rum Syrup

1 cup	granulated sugar	250 mL
1/2 cup	water	125 mL
3/4 cup	orange juice	175 mL
1/3 cup	dark rum	75 mL

1. Cake: Measure ingredients into machine's baking pan in the order recommended by the manufacturer. Insert pan into the oven chamber. Select **Dough Cycle**.

2. With floured hands or with a rubber spatula, remove dough from baking pan and place directly into prepared pan. Cover and let rise in a warm, draft-free place for 45 to 60 minutes or until bubbly. Meanwhile, preheat oven to 350° F (180° C).

3. Rum syrup: In a small saucepan over medium-high heat, combine sugar and water. Bring to a boil and cook for 1 minute. Remove from heat and stir in orange juice and rum; set aside.

4. Bake cake in preheated oven for 30 to 35 minutes. Tip the baba from the pan onto a large plate. Leave upside down. Immediately, with a long wooden skewer, poke numerous holes into the cake. Slowly spoon the rum syrup over the cake, letting it soak in. Let stand for at least 2 hours before serving.

*I*n the Baltic countries of of Latvia, Lithuania and Estonia, this saffron-flavored fruit bread is traditionally served at birthday celebrations. But you can enjoy it anytime.

Tip

Soaking the saffron threads in boiling water ensures a strong saffron flavor and a deep yellow color.

Variation

To personalize this bread, form the dough into the celebrant's initial — or number of years.

Baltic Birthday Bread

Makes 1 loaf

Baking sheet, lightly greased

Bread

1/4 cup	boiling water	50 mL
1 tsp	saffron threads	5 mL
1 cup	milk (room temperature)	250 mL
1 1/4 tsp	salt	6 mL
3 tbsp	honey	45 mL
2 tbsp	butter	25 mL
3 1/2 cups	bread flour	875 mL
1/2 cup	raisins	125 mL
1/2 cup	slivered almonds	125 mL
1/4 cup	candied mixed peel	50 mL
1 1/2 tsp	bread machine yeast	7 mL

Almond Finish

1	egg yolk	1
1 tbsp	water	15 mL
1/4 cup	sliced almonds	50 mL

1. In a bowl combine boiling water and saffron; cool to room temperature. Place in bread machine baking pan. Measure remaining ingredients into baking pan in the order recommended by the manufacturer. Insert pan into the oven chamber. Select **Dough Cycle**.

2. Remove dough to a lightly floured surface. Cover with a large bowl and let rest for 10 to 15 minutes. Form into a 30-inch (75 cm) rope. Place on prepared baking sheet, shaping into a figure "8". Tuck the ends under at the point of intersection. Cover and let rise in a warm, draft-free place for 30 to 45 minutes or until doubled in volume. Meanwhile, preheat oven to 375° F (190° C).

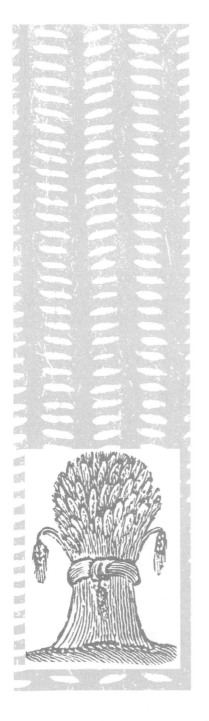

3. In a small bowl, whisk together egg yolk and water until smooth. Brush the risen dough with the glaze and sprinkle with sliced almonds. Bake in preheated oven for 35 to 40 minutes or until bread sounds hollow when tapped on the bottom.

This variation of traditional German kaffeekuchen (or coffee cake) is ideal served for breakfast or dessert.

Tip

Spread the filling right to the edge of the dough. Place the springform pans on baking sheets to catch any overflow in the oven.

Variation

For two different desserts, reduce the cranberry filling by half and use for only one of the cakes. For the second cake, use any filling you like — or try the filling from BLUEBERRY PEACH STREUSEL CAKE (see recipe, page 102), using half the quantity given in the recipe.

Cranberry Walnut Kaffeekuchen

Makes 2 cakes

Two 10-inch (3 L) springform pans, lightly greased

Cake

1/2 cup	water	125 mL
1/2 cup	fresh orange juice	125 mL
2 tsp	orange zest	10 mL
1	egg	1
1 1/2 tsp	salt	7 mL
1/4 cup	granulated sugar	50 mL
2 tbsp	butter	25 mL
3 cups	bread flour	750 mL
1/3 cup	buttermilk powder	75 mL
1/2 tsp	ground allspice	2 mL
1 1/2 tsp	bread machine yeast	7 mL

Cranberry Filling

3 cups	fresh cranberries	750 mL
1 cup	maple syrup	250 mL

Walnut Topping

2/3 cup	granulated sugar	150 mL
2/3 cup	all-purpose flour	150 mL
4 tsp	orange zest	20 mL
2 tsp	ground ginger	10 mL
1/2 cup	butter	125 mL
2 cups	chopped walnuts	500 mL

1. Cake: Measure ingredients into baking pan in the order recommended by the manufacturer. Insert pan into the oven chamber. Select **Dough Cycle**.

2. Filling: In a saucepan combine cranberries and maple syrup. Bring to a boil. Simmer for 4 to 6 minutes or until the cranberries open. Remove from heat; set aside.

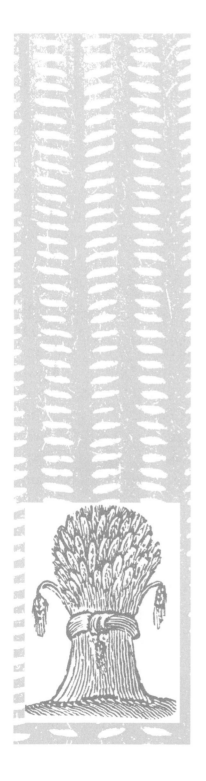

3. Topping: In a large bowl, combine sugar, flour, zest and ginger. With a pastry blender, cut in the butter until crumbly. Add walnuts; set aside.

4. Remove dough to a lightly floured surface. Cover with a large bowl and let rest for 10 to 15 minutes. Divide dough in half. Press one portion of the dough into one of the prepared pans. Top with half the cranberry filling and sprinkle with half the walnut topping. Repeat with the second pan. Cover and let rise in a warm, draft-free place for 45 to 60 minutes or until doubled in volume. Meanwhile, preheat oven to 350° F (180° C).

5. Bake in preheated oven for 40 to 45 minutes or until kaffeekuchen is golden brown. Serve warm or cold.

Here's a traditional soda bread with the great flavor and texture of raisins and caraway seeds, all updated for the bread machine.

Tip

Break up any lumps in the baking soda and mix with the flour before adding the yeast. Don't add more baking soda than is called for here or the bread will end up with a bitter aftertaste.

Yes, you're reading it right: The 1.5 lb (750 g) recipe contains *more* yeast than the 2 lb (1 kg).

Variation

For a different flavor combination, replace the raisins and caraway seeds with dates and anise seeds. The recipe also works with both ingredients omitted — although your bread will be "freckle-less"!

Irish Freckle Bread

1.5 LB (750 G)

1 1/4 cups	water	300 mL
1 1/2 tsp	salt	7 mL
2 tbsp	granulated sugar	25 mL
2 tbsp	shortening	25 mL
3 cups	bread flour	750 mL
1/3 cup	buttermilk powder	75 mL
1/4 tsp	baking soda	1 mL
2 tsp	caraway seeds	10 mL
1 1/2 tsp	bread machine yeast	7 mL
1/2 cup	raisins	125 mL

2 LB (1 KG)

1 1/2 cups	water	375 mL
1 3/4 tsp	salt	8 mL
3 tbsp	granulated sugar	45 mL
2 tbsp	shortening	25 mL
3 1/2 cups	bread flour	800 mL
1/2 cup	buttermilk powder	125 mL
1/4 tsp	baking soda	1 mL
1 tbsp	caraway seeds	15 mL
1 1/4 tsp	bread machine yeast	6 mL
3/4 cup	raisins	175 mL

1. Measure all ingredients *except raisins* into baking pan in the order recommended by the manufacturer. Insert pan into the oven chamber. Select **Basic Cycle**. Add raisins at the "add ingredient" signal.

These traditional East European pastry treats are great to pack in a lunch or serve as an after-school snack.

Tip

Make sure the rims of the dough circles are slightly higher than the centers or the filling will spill over.

Just before filling, press the center of each circle flat, using the bottom of a flour-coated glass.

Variation

Try making Kolach Bundles: Roll the dough into 3-inch (7.5 cm) squares. Place 1 tbsp (15 mL) filling in the center of each square. Pull the opposite corners over the dough and tuck in the loose ends.

Try the date filling from the recipe for DATE ORANGE BUNDLES(see page 106).

Kolaches

Makes 24 kolaches

Baking sheets, lightly greased

Kolaches

1 1/4 cups	water	300 mL
1	egg	1
1 1/2 tsp	salt	7 mL
3 tbsp	honey	45 mL
2 tbsp	shortening	25 mL
4 cups	bread flour	1000 mL
1/3 cup	buttermilk powder	75 mL
1 tsp	bread machine yeast	5 mL

Mincemeat Filling

1 1/2 cups	prepared mincemeat	375 mL
2 tbsp	dark rum	25 mL

1. Measure kolach ingredients into baking pan in the order recommended by the manufacturer. Insert pan into the oven chamber. Select **Dough Cycle**.

2. Filling: In a small bowl, combine mincemeat and rum; set aside. Remove dough to a lightly floured surface. Cover with a large bowl and let rest for 10 to 15 minutes. Divide dough into 24 portions. Form into balls. Flatten into 2 1/2-inch (6 cm) circles, leaving a 1/4-inch (5 mm) rim. Spoon 1 tbsp (15 mL) filling in the center of each. Place kolaches 1 inch (2.5 cm) apart on prepared baking sheets. Cover and let rise in a warm, draft-free place for 30 to 45 minutes or until doubled in volume. Meanwhile, preheat oven to 350° F (180° C).

3. Bake in preheated oven for 20 to 25 minutes or until kolaches sound hollow when tapped on the bottom.

This soft-textured loaf is packed with all the great flavors of Mediterranean cuisine — garlic, olives, feta cheese and oregano.

Tip

To save time, buy pitted, sliced Kalamata olives.

Be sure the feta cheese is well drained before crumbling.

Yes, you're reading it right: The 1.5 lb (750 g) recipe contains the *same* amount of yeast as the 2 lb (1 kg).

Variation

Substitute 3 tbsp (45 mL) fresh basil for the oregano.

Mediterranean Bread

1.5 LB (750 G)

1 cup	water	250 mL
1/3 cup	crumbled feta cheese	75 mL
3	cloves garlic, minced	3
1 1/4 tsp	salt	6 mL
1 tbsp	honey	15 mL
1 tbsp	olive oil	15 mL
3 1/4 cups	bread flour	800 mL
1/2 cup	sliced Kalamata olives	125 mL
2 tsp	dried oregano	10 mL
3/4 tsp	bread machine yeast	4 mL

2 LB (1 KG)

1 1/4 cups	water	300 mL
1/2 cup	crumbled feta cheese	125 mL
4	cloves garlic, minced	4
1 1/2 tsp	salt	7 mL
1 tbsp	honey	15 mL
2 tbsp	olive oil	25 mL
4 cups	bread flour	1050 mL
3/4 cup	sliced Kalamata olives	175 mL
1 tbsp	dried oregano	15 mL
3/4 tsp	bread machine yeast	4 mL

1. Measure ingredients into baking pan in the order recommended by the manufacturer. Insert pan into the oven chamber. Select **Basic Cycle**.

*H*ere's a traditional German treat that your kids will love — twists of yeast dough, deep-fried, then dusted with confectioner's sugar. The name comes from the German word raeder (wheels), which refers to the cutting wheels used to shape the dough.

Tip

Oil can become bitter if heated too long in the deep-fryer. Start heating only when you are ready to fry the twists.

Variation

Dust warm twists with sifted confectioner's sugar, instead of lemon glaze.

Radar Kuchen

Makes 18 twists

Baking sheet, lightly greased

1 cup	water	250 mL
2	eggs	2
1/4 cup	nonfat dry milk	50 mL
1 1/2 tsp	salt	7 mL
1/4 cup	granulated sugar	50 mL
1/4 cup	shortening	50 mL
4 cups	bread flour	1000 mL
2 tsp	bread machine yeast	10 mL

Lemon Glaze

1 cup	sifted confectioner's sugar	250 mL
1 tbsp	lemon juice	15 mL
1 tbsp	water	15 mL

1. Measure ingredients into baking pan in the order recommended by the manufacturer. Insert pan into the oven chamber. Select **Dough Cycle**.

2. Remove dough to a lightly floured surface. Cover with a large bowl and let rest for 10 to 15 minutes. Divide dough in half. Roll out each half to a 9- by 8-inch (22.5 by 20 cm) rectangle. Cut the dough into 3- by 2-inch (7.5 by 5 cm) rectangles. Cut a 1 1/2-inch (3 cm) slit lengthwise down the center of each rectangle. Tuck one end into the slit, gently pulling the end part-way through. Cover and let rise in a warm, draft-free place for 30 to 45 minutes or until doubled in volume.

3. Preheat deep fryer to 350° F (180° C). Deep-fry the kuchen for 30 to 40 seconds per side or until golden-brown. Drain on paper towels.

4. Glaze: In a bowl combine confectioner's sugar, lemon juice and water; mix until smooth. Drizzle over kuchen.

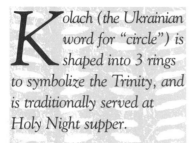

olach (the Ukrainian word for "circle") is shaped into 3 rings to symbolize the Trinity, and is traditionally served at Holy Night supper.

Tip

Stack baked rings with the largest on the bottom and insert a long taper candle through the center.

Variation

To make one large braid, make only first batch of dough.

Ukrainian Egg Bread (Kolach)

Makes one 3-ring tiered braid

Two baking sheets, lightly greased

Bread (Batch 1)

3/4 cup	water	175 mL
2	eggs	2
1 1/4 tsp	salt	6 mL
2 tbsp	granulated sugar	25 mL
2 tbsp	butter	25 mL
3 1/4 cups	bread flour	800 mL
1 1/4 tsp	bread machine yeast	6 mL
1/4 cup	milk	50 mL

Bread (Batch 2)

3/4 cup	water	175 mL
2	eggs	2
1 1/4 tsp	salt	6 mL
2 tbsp	granulated sugar	25 mL
2 tbsp	butter	25 mL
3 1/4 cups	bread flour	800 mL
1 1/4 tsp	bread machine yeast	6 mL
1/4 cup	milk	50 mL

1. Measure Batch 1 ingredients *except milk* into machine's baking pan in the order recommended by the manufacturer. Insert pan into the oven chamber. Select **Dough Cycle**.

2. Remove dough to a lightly floured surface. Cover with a large bowl and let rest for 10 to 15 minutes. Divide dough into 3 portions. Roll each into a 28-inch (75 cm) rope. Braid the 3 ropes. Form into a circle, pinching ends together. Place on prepared baking sheet. Cover and let rise in a warm, draft-free place for 30 to 45 minutes or until doubled in volume.

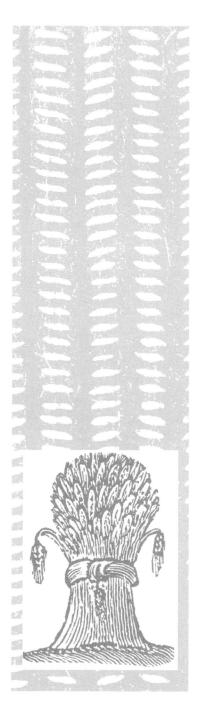

3. Repeat Steps 1 and 2 with Batch 2 ingredients.

4. Preheat oven to 350° F (180° C). Brush the ring from Batch 1 with milk. Bake in preheated oven for 10 minutes, then brush with milk a second time. Bake for another 15 to 20 minutes or until ring sounds hollow when tapped on the bottom.

5. Divide dough from Batch 2 into 2 portions, one twice as large as the other. Using the larger portion, divide dough into 3 portions; roll each into a 21-inch (55 cm) rope. Braid the 3 ropes. Form into a circle, pinching ends together. Divide remaining dough into 3 portions; roll each into a 14-inch (35 cm) rope. Braid the 3 ropes. Form into a circle, pinching ends together. Place at least 2 inches (5 cm) apart on prepared baking sheet. Cover and let rise in a warm, draft-free place for 30 to 45 minutes or until doubled in volume.

6. Brush the rings from Batch 2 with milk. Bake in preheated oven for 10 minutes, then brush with milk a second time. Bake for 10 to 15 minutes or until rings sound hollow when tapped on the bottom.

7. Stack cooled rings, with the largest ring on the bottom. Insert a long taper candle through the center of the three rings.

*T*hanks to Suzel Donitz of Canmore, Alberta, for suggesting this Walliser-style bread. The ingredients here are used in the same proportions as at her local bakery.

Tip

Because it contains neither fat nor sugar to provide food for the yeast, this loaf is heavier than most, but still fine-textured and delicious.

For instructions on cooking rye groats, see Techniques Glossary, page 183.

Yes, you're reading it right: The 1.5 lb (750 g) recipe contains the *same* amount of yeast as the 2 lb (1 kg).

Variation

For a richer loaf, use a dark rye flour and substitute cold coffee for some or all of the water.

Swiss Rye Loaf

1.5 LB (750 G)

1 1/4 cups	water	300 mL
1 1/4 tsp	salt	6 mL
3/4 cup	whole-wheat flour	175 mL
2 cups	bread flour	500 mL
1/2 cup	rye flour	125 mL
1/3 cup	gluten	75 mL
1 cup	cooked rye groats	250 mL
1 tbsp	bread machine yeast	15 mL

2 LB (1 KG)

1 1/2 cups	water	375 mL
1 3/4 tsp	salt	8 mL
1 cup	whole-wheat flour	250 mL
2 1/4 cups	bread flour	550 mL
3/4 cup	rye flour	175 mL
1/3 cup	gluten	75 mL
1 cup	cooked rye groats	250 mL
1 tbsp	bread machine yeast	15 mL

1. Measure ingredients into baking pan in the order recommended by the manufacturer. Insert pan into the oven chamber. Select **Whole Wheat Cycle**.

DATE ORANGE BUNDLES (PAGE 106) ➤

OVERLEAF: SUMMER SUNFLOWER (PAGE 144)

SHAPES FOR EVERY OCCASION
(FOR THE KID IN YOU)

TIPS FOR MAKING PERFECT SHAPES EVERY TIME 130

CHOCOLATE RASPBERRY DANISH 131

THREE LITTLE PIGGIES 132

FRIENDLY FROSTY 134

CIRCLE OF LIGHT 136

PEANUT BUTTER BANANA SWIRL LOAF 137

PECAN CRISPS 138

PUMPERNICKEL TURBAN 140

SOUP-IN-A-BREAD-BOWL 142

SUMMER SUNFLOWER 144

VALENTINE CHOCOLATE SWEETHEART BREAD 146

SOFT PRETZELS 148

Here's where bread making really gets fun.
Try these recipes with your kids. Everyone will enjoy shaping the
dough — as well as seeing (and eating!) the finished product.

◄ BALTIC BIRTHDAY BREAD (PAGE 118)

TIPS FOR MAKING PERFECT SHAPES EVERY TIME

- Follow the recipe instructions exactly. The quality of the finished product will depend on exact sizes, thicknesses and baking times.

- Measure lengths with a steel or plastic (not wooden) ruler. Wash it in the dishwasher between uses.

- Make all cuts using sharp scissors rather than a knife; this prevents the dough from being flattened.

- Work with one portion of dough at a time. Keep the remaining portions covered to prevent them from drying out.

- When making wreaths or braids, tuck all ends under; this helps to retain the desired shape during baking.

- For filled shapes, seal all seams and place dough seam-side down on the baking sheet. This holds the filling inside the dough during baking and prevents undesirable cracks from forming.

- In filled, rolled breads such as PEANUT BUTTER BANANA SWIRL LOAF (see recipe, page 137), there is a tendency for large air bubbles to form under the top crust. To help prevent this (and the dough separating from the filling), poke several holes through the risen loaf with a long wooden skewer.

- To ensure that shapes don't disappear while baking, check after 10 to 15 minutes in the oven. If the features of the shapes have disappeared, remove the product from the oven and quickly re-cut or re-poke the shape to sharpen the features. Continue baking until done, then loosen the shapes from the baking sheet immediately. Use a long flat metal spatula to slide the baked shapes onto a large rack to cool completely.

This not-too-sweet breakfast treat will tempt even the fussiest eater. The chocolate-orange combination is irresistible served warm from the oven.

Tip

Pour icing or chocolate syrup into a squeeze bottle to drizzle across the warm Danish.

Variation

Kids enjoy making Danish into fun shapes. For instructions on shaping, see Techniques Glossary, page 183.

Chocolate Raspberry Danish

Makes 12 Danish

Baking sheet, lightly greased

1 1/3 cups	water	325 mL
3 tbsp	thawed frozen orange juice concentrate	45 mL
1 1/2 tsp	salt	7 mL
3 tbsp	granulated sugar	45 mL
3 tbsp	butter	45 mL
4 1/2 cups	bread flour	1125 mL
1/4 cup	unsweetened cocoa	50 mL
1 tsp	bread machine yeast	5 mL
1/4 cup	raspberry jam	50 mL

1. Measure ingredients *except raspberry jam* into baking pan in the order recommended by the manufacturer. Insert pan into the oven chamber. Select **Dough Cycle**.

2. Remove dough to a lightly floured surface. Cover with a large bowl and let rest for 10 to 15 minutes. Roll out the dough into a 16- by 12-inch (40 by 30 cm) rectangle. Cut into 12 strips, each 1 inch (2.5 cm) wide and 16 inches (40 cm) long.

3. On prepared baking sheet, beginning in the center, coil each strip into a circle, keeping the dough strips 1/4 inch (5 mm) apart. Tuck the ends under. Cover and let rise in a warm, draft-free place for 30 to 45 minutes or until doubled in volume. Meanwhile, preheat oven to 375° F (190° C).

4. Spread each center with 1/2 to 1 tsp (2 to 5 mL) raspberry jam. Bake for 20 to 30 minutes or until Danish sound hollow when tapped on the bottom.

These nursery-rhyme characters are a great favorite in our house. Kids will have as much fun making them as eating them.

Tip

Check the piggies after 10 minutes of baking. If an ear or a tail needs to be repositioned, remove the baking sheet from the oven and gently (but quickly), move the piece(s) back into place.

Variation

Make piggie sandwiches: Carefully slice the piggies horizontally and fill with your choice of sandwich ingredients.

Three Little Piggies

Makes 3 piggies

Two baking sheets, lightly greased

1 1/2 cups	water	375 mL
1/4 cup	nonfat dry milk	50 mL
1 1/4 tsp	salt	6 mL
3 tbsp	packed brown sugar	45 mL
3 tbsp	shortening	45 mL
1 1/2 cups	whole-wheat flour	375 mL
2 1/4 cups	bread flour	550 mL
1 1/2 tsp	bread machine yeast	7 mL
6	raisins	6

1. Measure ingredients *except raisins* into baking pan in the order recommended by the manufacturer. Insert pan into the oven chamber. Select **Dough Cycle**.

2. Remove dough to a lightly floured surface. Cover with a large bowl and let rest for 10 to 15 minutes. Divide dough into 10 portions. While making and assembling the "piggy parts," keep any dough you're not working with covered.

3. Heads: Roll out 3 portions into 5-inch (12.5 cm) circles. Place 1 circle on the center of a prepared baking sheet and the remaining circles well-spaced on the other prepared baking sheet.

4. Ears: Pat 3 portions into 4- by 3-inch (10 by 7.5 cm) rectangles. Cut each in half diagonally to make 6 triangles. Tuck the short side of each triangle under the top of the heads, cut-side facing out. Fold the ends over, towards the center of the heads, to make typical floppy pig ears.

5. Hooves: Cut 2 portions into 3 pieces each. Form into 6 teardrop shapes. With a sharp knife, cut a small slit in the side of the teardrop to form a cloven hoof. Tuck the hooves securely, under the bottom of the head.

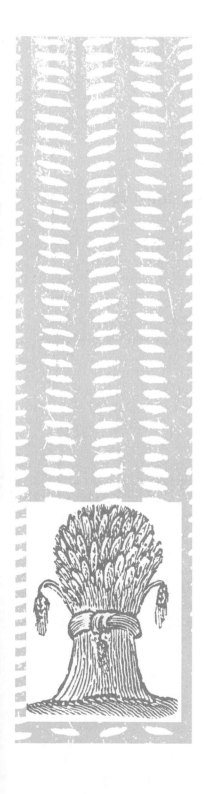

6. Tails: Cut 1 portion into 3 pieces. Roll each into a long, thin 8-inch (20 cm) rope. Curl, then place between the ears, tucking one end under the head to secure.

7. Snouts: Divide the last portion into 3 pieces. Roll out each to a 2-inch (5 cm) circle. Position on the center of each head. Poke 2 fingers deep into the center to form nostrils. Add raisins for eyes.

8. Cover and let assembled dough shapes rise in a warm, draft-free place for 30 to 45 minutes or until doubled in volume. Meanwhile, preheat oven to 350° F (180° C).

9. When dough has risen, poke the nostrils again. Bake in preheated oven for 20 to 30 minutes or until piggies sound hollow when tapped on the bottom.

This jolly fellow isn't made from snow — but light, fluffy dough. What child (or grown-up) can resist?

Tip

After 10 to 15 minutes in the oven, check Frosty to make sure his parts and decorations are still in place. If not, remove from the oven and adjust as necessary.

Variation

After you've finished baking and allowed Frosty to cool, you and your young helpers can add further decorations — such as licorice pipe, a carrot nose and a narrow scarf.

Friendly Frosty

Baking sheet, lightly greased

Bread

1 1/2 cups	milk	375 mL
1 tsp	salt	5 mL
1/4 cup	granulated sugar	50 mL
3 tbsp	butter	45 mL
3 3/4 cups	bread flour	925 mL
1 1/2 tsp	bread machine yeast	7 mL

Finishing Touches

2	raisins	2
1	rope licorice	1
4	chocolate chips	4

1. Measure bread ingredients into machine's baking pan in the order recommended by the manufacturer. Insert pan into the oven chamber. Select **Dough Cycle**.

2. Remove dough to a lightly floured surface. Cover with a large bowl and let rest for 10 to 15 minutes. Divide dough into 4 portions, making 2 portions slightly larger.

3. Body: Form the 2 larger portions of dough into a 6-inch (15 cm) and a 5-inch (12.5 cm) circle, slightly flattened on one side. Place with flattened sides touching and with larger circle at the bottom of prepared baking sheet. Seal seam.

4. Head: Form 1 portion of the dough into a 4-inch (10 cm) slightly rounded circle. Place on baking sheet, touching the 5-inch (12.5 cm) circle, to form the snowman. Seal seam.

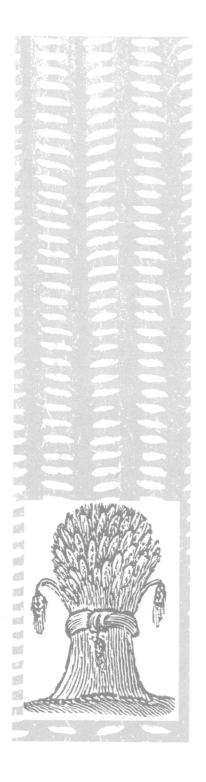

5. Hat: Roll out remaining portion of the dough into a 5-inch (12.5 cm) square. Cut 1 inch (2.5 cm) off one side and lengthen to 6 inches (15 cm) to form the brim. Place the brim on the head of the snowman on an angle. Place the square over the brim.

6. Finish touches: Add raisins for eyes, rope licorice for a mouth and a row of chocolate chips for buttons. Cover and let rise in a warm, draft-free place for 30 to 45 minutes or until doubled in volume. Meanwhile, preheat oven to 350° F (180° C).

7. Bake in preheated oven for 30 to 40 minutes or until Frosty sounds hollow when tapped on the bottom.

*L*et flickering candle-light cast a warm glow over your family gathering this Thanksgiving. Revive an old custom and decorate your table with this braided centerpiece.

Tip

Check indents in the bread after 15 minutes of baking. If holes have closed, quickly enlarge to the correct size with the base of the candle. Continue baking.

Air-drying may take up to 2 weeks in hot, humid climates.

To preserve centerpiece, apply 2 coats of shellac, allowing to dry completely between coats.

Variation

Taper each rope slightly at the ends before braiding, then leave the braid in a long loaf resembling a Challah.

Circle of Light

Makes 1 braided centerpiece

Baking sheet, lightly greased
3 or 5 dripless candles

1 1/2 cups	water	375 mL
1 1/4 tsp	salt	6 mL
1 tbsp	granulated sugar	15 mL
2 tbsp	shortening	25 mL
4 1/2 cups	bread flour	1125 mL
1 1/4 tsp	bread machine yeast	6 mL

1. Measure ingredients into baking pan in the order recommended by the manufacturer. Insert pan into the oven chamber. Select **Dough Cycle**.

2. Remove dough to a lightly floured surface. Cover with a large bowl and let rest for 10 to 15 minutes. Divide dough into 3 portions. Roll each with the palm of your hand into a long, smooth rope 1 inch (2.5 cm) in diameter. Braid all three together. Form braid into a circle. Pinch ends to seal. Place on prepared baking sheet.

3. Wrap a square of foil around the base of each candle. Push the candles in between the ropes of the dough, at evenly spaced intervals, tucking them deep so they won't be pushed out when the dough rises. Cover and let rise in a warm, draft-free place for 30 to 40 minutes or until doubled in volume. Meanwhile, preheat oven to 350° F (180° C).

4. Remove candles, leaving the foil in the dough. Bake in preheated oven for 40 to 45 minutes or until the braid sounds hollow when tapped on the bottom. Air dry completely on a cooling rack before using as a centerpiece.

Remember how much you loved peanut butter and banana sandwiches when you were a kid? Bring back the memories with this loaf served warm from the oven in thick slices with a glass of milk.

Tip

If the top of this loaf is browned after 30 minutes of baking, but the bottom is still too light and soft, remove the loaf from the pan and set it directly on the oven rack to brown for the last few minutes of baking.

Variation

Pancake syrup (either light or regular) or packed brown sugar can be substituted for the maple syrup.

For a milder flavor add 1 to 2 tbsp (15 to 25 mL) mashed banana to the filling.

Peanut Butter Banana Swirl Loaf

Makes 1 loaf

9- by 5-inch (2 L) loaf pan, lightly greased

Loaf

1/2 cup	water	125 mL
1 cup	mashed ripe banana	250 mL
1/4 cup	nonfat dry milk	50 mL
3/4 tsp	salt	4 mL
3 tbsp	maple syrup	45 mL
2 tbsp	butter	25 mL
3 1/3 cups	bread flour	825 mL
2 tsp	bread machine yeast	10 mL

Peanut Butter Filling

1/2 cup	peanut butter	125 mL
1/3 cup	packed brown sugar	75 mL
1/2 cup	unsalted peanuts	125 mL

1. Measure loaf ingredients into machine's baking pan in the order recommended by the manufacturer. Insert pan into the oven chamber. Select **Dough Cycle**.

2. Filling: In a bowl, combine peanut butter and brown sugar. Set aside.

3. Remove dough to a lightly floured surface. Cover with a large bowl and let rest for 10 to 15 minutes. Roll out to an 18- by 8-inch (45 by 20 cm) rectangle. Spread the filling to within 1/2 inch (1 cm) of edges. Sprinkle with peanuts. Beginning at short side, roll jellyroll style. Tuck ends under. Place, seam-side down, in prepared loaf pan. Cover and let rise in a warm, draft-free place for 30 to 45 minutes or until doubled in volume. Meanwhile, preheat oven to 350° F (180° C).

4. With a long skewer, poke several holes through the risen dough. Bake in preheated oven for 40 to 50 minutes or until bread sounds hollow when tapped on the bottom.

Take these crunchy treats to work and set them out to share during coffee break. Just don't mention the calories!

Tip

Be sure to follow the instructions to cover the rolls with waxed paper before rolling. Otherwise the dough will stick to the rolling pin.

Variation

Bake these crisps muffin-style: place the twelve 1-inch (2.5 cm) slices in individual cups of a muffin tin (no need to roll). Cover and let rise until doubled in volume. Bake as directed.

Pecan Crisps

Makes 24 crisps

Baking sheet, lightly greased

Crisps

1 cup	milk	250 mL
1	egg	1
1 1/4 tsp	salt	6 mL
3 tbsp	granulated sugar	45 mL
1/4 cup	butter	50 mL
3 3/4 cups	bread flour	925 mL
1/2 tsp	cinnamon	2 mL
1 1/2 tsp	bread machine yeast	7 mL

Cinnamon Filling

1/4 cup	butter, melted	50 mL
1/2 cup	packed brown sugar	125 mL
1/2 cup	granulated sugar	125 mL
1 tsp	cinnamon	5 mL

Pecan Topping

2/3 cup	granulated sugar	150 mL
2/3 cup	chopped pecans	150 mL
1 tsp	cinnamon	5 mL
2 tbsp	butter, melted and cooled	25 mL

1. Measure crisps ingredients into machine's baking pan in the order recommended by the manufacturer. Insert pan into the oven chamber. Select **Dough Cycle**.

2. Filling: In a small bowl, combine melted butter, brown sugar, granulated sugar and cinnamon. Set aside.

3. Topping: In another small bowl, combine granulated sugar, pecans and cinnamon. Set aside.

4. Remove dough to a lightly floured surface. Cover with a large bowl and let rest for 10 to 15 minutes. Divide dough in half. Roll each half into a 12-inch (30 cm) square. Spread each with half the filling, right to the edges. Beginning at the long side, roll jelly-roll style. Pinch to seal seams. Cut each into twelve 1-inch (2.5 cm) slices. Place cut-side up on prepared baking sheet, at least 3 inches (7.5 cm) apart.

5. Cover slices with a sheet of waxed paper. Flatten with a rolling pin until 1/8 inch (2 mm) thick. Brush with cooled butter and sprinkle with pecan topping. Cover with waxed paper and re-roll lightly with a rolling pin. Meanwhile, preheat oven to 400° F (220° C).

6. Bake in preheated oven for 10 to 15 minutes or until crisps are golden brown.

Our inspiration for this seed-studded turban shape originally came from King Arthur's "Baker's Store" in Norwich, VT. Its outstanding visual appeal makes this a perfect centerpiece for a gourmet dinner.

Tip

Use the seeds and grains as given in the recipe, or choose others to provide a variety of different colors and textures.

Variation

To bake as a hearth bread without the seeds, let the dough double in volume before baking. Cut into wedges and serve.

Pumpernickel Turban

Makes 1 turban

Preheat oven to 375° F (190° C)
Baking sheet, lightly greased

Bread

1 1/4 cups	coffee (room temperature)	300 mL
2 tbsp	vinegar	25 mL
1 tsp	salt	5 mL
1/4 cup	molasses	50 mL
2 tbsp	shortening	25 mL
1 1/3 cups	whole-wheat flour	325 mL
1 1/4 cups	bread flour	300 mL
2/3 cup	rye flour	150 mL
1/3 cup	buttermilk powder	75 mL
2 tbsp	unsweetened cocoa	25 mL
1 1/4 tsp	bread machine yeast	6 mL

Seed Topping

3	egg yolks	3
1/4 cup	sunflower seeds	50 mL
1/4 cup	caraway seeds	50 mL
1/4 cup	sesame seeds	50 mL
1/4 cup	fennel seeds	50 mL
1/4 cup	millet meal	50 mL
1/4 cup	flaxseeds	50 mL
1/4 cup	12-grain cereal	50 mL
1/4 cup	poppy seeds	50 mL
1/4 cup	oat bran	50 mL
1/4 cup	pumpkin seeds	50 mL
1/4 cup	anise seeds	50 mL
1/4 cup	millet	50 mL

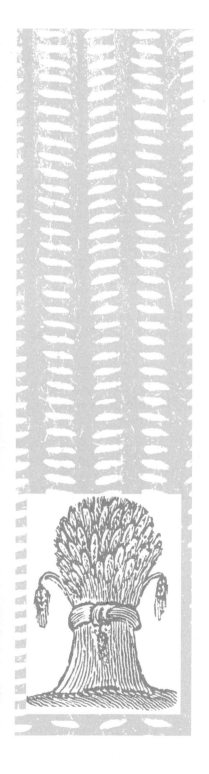

1. Measure bread ingredients into machine's baking pan in the order recommended by the manufacturer. Insert pan into the oven chamber. Select **Dough Cycle.**

2. Remove dough to a lightly floured surface. Cover with a large bowl and let rest for 10 to 15 minutes. Form into an 8-inch (20 cm) dome, 2 to 2 1/2 inches (5 to 6 cm) high in the center.

3. From a piece of paper, cut out a 7-inch (17.5 cm) circle. Fold the paper to form 12 equal sections. Gently set on the center of dome. With scissors, make 1/4-inch (5 mm) cuts at the edge of the dough to mark each fold. With a pastry wheel and using a ruler as a guide, connect the cuts making 6 intersecting lines, each 1/8 inch (2 mm) deep. Cut out one wedge from the pattern. Use the "open" wedge of the pattern as the guide to keep the seeds in the correct location.

4. Brush exposed wedges of dough with egg yolk and sprinkle with sunflower seeds, covering exposed area completely. Move the pattern to the next wedge and repeat with the next seed or grain. Continue until the entire dome is covered with topping. Bake in preheated oven for 30 to 35 minutes or until turban sounds hollow when tapped on the bottom.

*H*ate to do the dishes? Then this is the recipe for you. After enjoying the hearty soup, just eat the bowl!

Tip

To ensure the bowls are deep enough to hold the soup, form the dough into high, well-rounded balls. Each bowl should hold 2/3 to 3/4 cup (150 to 175 mL) of soup.

Variation

Our GERMAN LENTIL SOUP (recipe follows) is ideal for filling these bowls. But any hearty soup will do.

Soup-in-a-Bread-Bowl

Makes 4 bowls

Baking sheet, lightly greased

1 1/2 cups	water	375 mL
1 1/2 tsp	salt	7 mL
3 tbsp	packed brown sugar	45 mL
3 tbsp	shortening	45 mL
2 cups	whole-wheat flour	500 mL
2 cups	bread flour	500 mL
3/4 cup	cracked wheat	175 mL
1/2 cup	buttermilk powder	125 mL
1 1/4 tsp	bread machine yeast	6 mL

1. Measure ingredients into baking pan in the order recommended by the manufacturer. Insert pan into the oven chamber. Select **Dough Cycle**.

2. Remove dough to a lightly floured surface. Cover with a large bowl and let rest for 10 to 15 minutes. Divide into 4 portions. Form into balls 3 1/2 inches (9 cm) in diameter and at least 2 1/2 inches (6 cm) high. Cover and let rise in a warm, draft-free place for 30 to 45 minutes or until doubled in volume. Meanwhile, preheat oven to 375° F (190° C).

3. Bake in preheated oven for 20 to 25 minutes. When cool, cut out the center, leaving at least a 1-inch (2.5 cm) thickness of bread on the bottom and the sides. Fill with hot soup (see recipe on facing page) and serve.

This recipe makes more than twice the amount of soup needed to fill 4 bowls. If you don't want the extra soup, just halve the recipe.

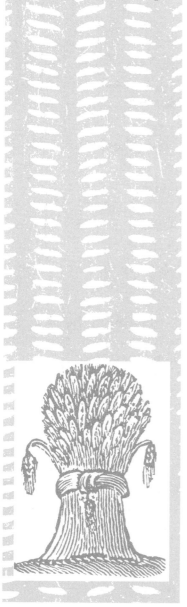

German Lentil Soup

5	slices bacon, diced	5
2	onions, sliced	2
2	carrots, sliced	2
2	stalks celery, sliced	2
1	ham bone	1
1 lb	lentils	500 g
1/2 tsp	freshly ground black pepper	2 mL
1/2 tsp	dried thyme	2 mL
2	bay leaves	2
10 cups	chicken stock	2.5 L
2 cups	chopped ham	500 mL
1 to 2 tbsp	lemon juice	15 to 25 mL

1. In a large frying pan over medium-high heat, cook bacon; remove with a slotted spoon and set aside. Return pan to heat and add onions, carrots and celery; sauté until tender but not browned.

2. In a large pot over medium heat, combine bacon, sautéed vegetables, ham bone, lentils, pepper, thyme, bay leaves and stock. Simmer for 1 hour or until lentils are tender. Remove bone and bay leaves. Add chopped ham. Add lemon juice just before serving.

osting a summer bridal shower? This golden sun-flower makes an unusual and attractive centerpiece for the buffet table.

Tip

To space "petals" evenly, imagine the face of a clock, and place petals at 12, 3, 6 and 9; then place remaining petals.

Variation

While sunflower is still hot from the oven, spoon a generous portion of apricot jam into the center of each petal.

Summer Sunflower

Baking sheet, lightly greased

Bread

1/2 cup	water	125 mL
1/4 cup	fresh orange juice	50 mL
2 tsp	orange zest	10 mL
2	eggs	2
1 1/4 tsp	salt	6 mL
1/4 cup	granulated sugar	50 mL
3 tbsp	butter	45 mL
3 3/4 cups	bread flour	925 mL
1 1/2 tsp	bread machine yeast	7 mL

Topping

1	egg yolk, lightly beaten	1
3 to 4 tbsp	sunflower seeds	45 to 60 mL
	Raspberry jam	

Orange Glaze

1 cup	sifted icing sugar	250 mL
2 tbsp	thawed frozen orange juice concentrate	25 mL

1. Measure ingredients into baking pan in the order recommended by the manufacturer. Insert pan into the oven chamber. Select **Dough Cycle**.

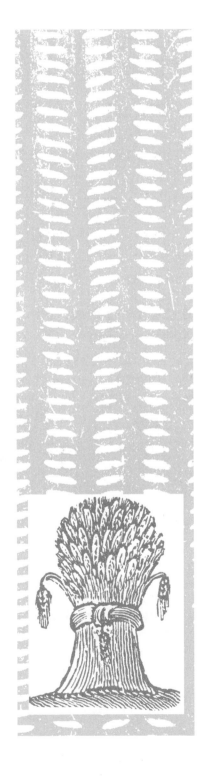

2. Remove dough to a lightly floured surface. Cover with a large bowl and let rest for 10 to 15 minutes. Roll out dough into a 12- by 9-inch (30 by 22.5 cm) rectangle. With a 3-inch (7.5 cm) donut cutter, cut into 12 donut shapes. Arrange 3 donut holes in the center of the prepared baking sheet, making sure the sides of the holes touch. Arrange the remaining 9 donut holes to form a ring around the center 3, making sure the sides of the donut holes touch. Place the donut shapes around the outside and touching the donut holes, stretching to form long, narrow sunflower-shaped petals. Brush the donut holes with egg yolk and generously sprinkle with sunflower seeds. Cover and let rise in a warm, draft-free place for 45 to 60 minutes or until doubled in volume. Meanwhile, preheat oven to 350° F (180° C).

3. Bake in preheated oven for 20 to 30 minutes or until sunflower sounds hollow when tapped on the bottom. While still hot, fill the petals with raspberry jam.

4. Glaze: In a small bowl, beat together sifted icing sugar and orange juice. Drizzle over the petals of the warm sunflower.

This rich, chocolatey heart is the perfect treat for Valentine's Day. But don't let that stop you from enjoying it anytime of the year.

Tip

Looking at the fudge-like consistency of this dough, it's hard to imagine that it will ever rise. But be patient — while the dough will take more time to double in volume, it's worth the wait.

Use regular (not spreadable) cream cheese for the filling.

Variation

Canned pears, well-drained and chopped, can be substituted for the fresh.

Valentine Chocolate Sweetheart Bread

Makes 1 loaf

Baking sheet, lightly greased

	Bread	
1/2 cup	milk (room temperature)	125 mL
1/4 cup	instant chocolate syrup	50 mL
2	eggs	2
1 tsp	salt	5 mL
1/4 cup	granulated sugar	50 mL
3 tbsp	butter	45 mL
3 1/4 cups	bread flour	800 mL
3 tbsp	unsweetened cocoa	45 mL
1 1/2 tsp	bread machine yeast	7 mL

	Pear and Cream Cheese Filling	
1	pkg (8 oz [250 g]) cream cheese, softened	1
3 or 4	fresh pears, chopped	3 or 4
2 to 3 tbsp	instant chocolate syrup	25 to 45 mL

1. Measure bread ingredients into baking pan in the order recommended by the manufacturer. Insert pan into the oven chamber. Select **Dough Cycle**.

2. Filling: In a small bowl, cream softened cream cheese. Set aside.

3. Remove dough to a lightly floured surface. Cover with a large bowl and let rest for 10 to 15 minutes. Roll out dough into a 22- by 8-inch (55 by 20 cm) rectangle. Spread with the cream cheese. Add chopped pears and drizzle with chocolate syrup.

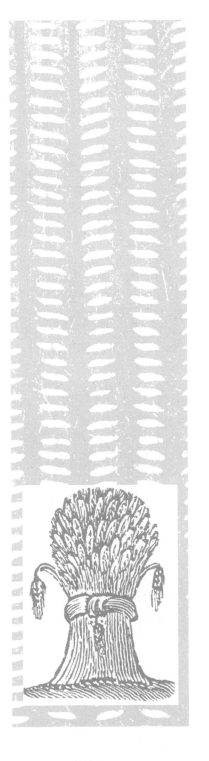

4. Beginning at the long side, roll jellyroll style. Pinch to seal seam. Place on prepared baking sheet, seam-side down, shaping into a heart. Pinch ends together. With scissors, along each side of the heart shape, cut down the center of dough, leaving 3 to 4 inches (7.5 by 10 cm) uncut at the top and bottom of the heart. Open the cut sections to show filling. Cover and let rise in a warm, draft-free place for 1 to 2 hours or until doubled in volume. Meanwhile, preheat oven to 350° F (180° C).

5. Bake in preheated oven for 35 to 40 minutes or until heart sounds hollow when tapped on the bottom.

*P*retzels like these are usually available only from big-city street vendors or at rural county fairs. Now you can make them at home with your bread machine.

Tip

Allowing the dough to rest for an extra 5 minutes makes it easier to handle.

Variation

For an authentic old world flavor, use beer (at room temperature) instead of water in the pretzel recipe.

Soft Pretzels

Makes 12 pretzels

Baking sheet, lightly greased

Pretzels

1 1/4 cups	water	300 mL
1 1/4 tsp	salt	6 mL
2 tbsp	granulated sugar	25 mL
1 tbsp	shortening	15 mL
4 cups	bread flour	1000 mL
1 tsp	bread machine yeast	5 mL

Topping

1	egg	1
1 tbsp	water	15 mL
1/4 cup	sesame seeds *or* sea salt	50 mL

1. Measure pretzel ingredients into baking pan in the order recommended by the manufacturer. Insert pan into the oven chamber. Select **Dough Cycle**.

2. Remove dough to a lightly floured surface. Cover with a large bowl and let rest for 10 to 15 minutes. Divide dough into 12 equal portions. Roll each into a 16-inch (40 cm) rope. On prepared baking sheet, form each rope into a circle. Grasping one end in each hand, cross the left end over the right and twist once, then bring the top of the circle over the twisted ends. Meanwhile, preheat oven to 350° F (180° C).

3. Topping: In a small bowl, whisk together egg and water. Brush unrisen dough with topping. Sprinkle with sesame seeds or salt. Bake in preheated oven for 20 to 25 minutes or until pretzels sound hollow when tapped on the bottom.

GLUTEN-FREE AND OTHER SPECIAL DIETARY BREADS

TIPS FOR BAKING GLUTEN-FREE BREADS   150

GLUTEN-FREE PUMPERNICKEL LOAF   151

GLUTEN-FREE STICKY BUNS   152

ANCIENT GRAINS BREAD   154

USING THE RAPID ONE- AND TWO-HOUR BASIC CYCLES   155

QUICK LOW-FAT HONEY FLAXSEED BREAD   156

SPELT BREAD   158

HIGH-FIBER CARROT BRAN BREAD   159

SUGAR-FREE APRICOT TEA RING   160

SEED-AND-SOY LOAF   162

Many people have health conditions (such as an allergy to the gluten in wheat flour) or nutritional concerns (such as reducing fat and sugar intake) that require special accommodation. These breads are designed to meet a variety of needs — and they taste great!

TIPS FOR BAKING GLUTEN-FREE BREADS

- Combine all the dry ingredients in a plastic bag or a large bowl before adding to the baking pan. Gluten-free flours have a fine, powder-like consistency, and require extra effort to make sure they don't lump, and that they mix properly with other ingredients.

- Mix eggs with the liquid ingredients in the bread machine for 2 to 3 minutes before adding the dry ingredients. This beats the eggs and distributes them in the liquids.

- To avoid lumps, add the dry ingredients slowly to the liquids while the machine is running.

- Scrape the corners, and the bottom of the baking pan as well as the kneading blade, for several minutes while adding the dry ingredients. Continue scraping until the dough is smooth and lump-free. This results in a better-textured loaf.

- Gluten-free dough needs vigorous mixing to ensure a high loaf. We found the kneading action of vertical-style machines is generally more effective than that of horizontal-style machines.

- Remove the kneading blade just after the long knead ends, but before the dough begins to rise. (This prevents over-kneading, which can result in a collapsed loaf.) Gluten-free dough is extremely sticky, so moisten your hands before removing the kneading blade from the baking pan.

- Resist the impulse to add more flour to gluten-free dough, even though it may resemble cake batter. Too much flour will produce a dry, crumbly loaf.

- When baking gluten-free loaves, don't add fruit at the "add ingredient" signal. Stirring in the fruit, by hand, at the end of kneading cycle, distributes it better.

- If your bread machine has a **Bake Cycle**, begin the loaf on **Dough Cycle**. Then, after the dough has risen, finish the loaf on **Bake**. This controls the amount of kneading, and eliminates the requirement for second knead (which results in a shorter loaf).

- Gluten-free loaves may be flat or slightly sunken. This is unavoidable since, without gluten, the dough does not trap the air that creates a rounded top.

With all the hearty flavor of traditional pumpernickel, this gluten-free version is great for sandwiches. Try it filled with sliced smoked turkey, accompanied by a crisp garlic dill pickle.

Tip

Before beginning this recipe, be sure to read the tips for gluten-free baking on page 150.

If your bread machine bakes both 1.5 lb (750 g) and 2 lb (1 kg) sizes, select the smaller loaf size for this recipe.

Variation

For a milder flavor, omit the coffee and unsweetened cocoa.

Gluten-Free Pumpernickel Loaf

1 1/2 tsp	salt	7 mL
3 tbsp	packed brown sugar	45 mL
2 cups	rice flour	500 mL
2/3 cup	potato starch	150 mL
1/3 cup	tapioca starch	75 mL
2 1/2 tsp	xanthan gum	12 mL
2 tsp	unsweetened cocoa	10 mL
1 1/2 tsp	instant coffee granules	7 mL
1/2 tsp	ground ginger	2 mL
1 tbsp	bread machine yeast	15 mL
3 tbsp	molasses	45 mL
1 1/2 cups	water (warmed to 98° F [37° C])	375 mL
1 tsp	cider vinegar	5 mL
2 tbsp	vegetable oil	25 mL
3	eggs, lightly beaten	3

1. Into a bowl or plastic bag, measure salt, brown sugar, rice flour, potato starch, tapioca starch, xanthan gum, cocoa, coffee granules, ginger and yeast. Mix well and set aside.

2. Into bread machine baking pan, measure molasses, water, vinegar and vegetable oil; add eggs. Insert pan into the oven chamber. Select **Rapid Two-Hour Basic Cycle**. Allow liquids to mix for approximately 2 minutes. Gradually add dry ingredients as bread machine is mixing. Scrape with rubber spatula while adding dry ingredients. Try to incorporate all dry ingredients within 1 to 2 minutes. When mixing and kneading are complete, leaving the bread pan in the bread machine, remove the kneading blade. Allow the bread machine to complete the cycle.

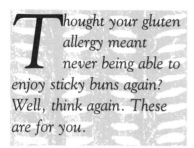

Thought your gluten allergy meant never being able to enjoy sticky buns again? Well, think again. These are for you.

Tip

Before beginning this recipe, be sure to read the tips for gluten-free baking on page 150.

For softer, moister, sticky buns, always serve them warm.

If you don't have two 8-inch (2 L) pans, use a single 9- by 13-inch (3 L) ungreased baking pan, and increase the baking time by 15 minutes.

Gluten-Free Sticky Buns

Makes 18 buns

Two 8-inch (2 L) square baking pans, ungreased

1 1/2 tsp	salt	7 mL
2 1/4 cups	rice flour	550 mL
2/3 cup	potato starch	150 mL
1/3 cup	tapioca starch	75 mL
2 1/2 tsp	xanthan gum	12 mL
1 tsp	ground cinnamon	5 mL
2 tsp	bread machine yeast	10 mL
1/2 cup	water (warmed to 98° F [37° C])	125 mL
1 tsp	cider vinegar	5 mL
1 cup	mashed banana	250 mL
1/4 cup	honey	50 mL
1/4 cup	butter, melted	50 mL
3	eggs, lightly beaten	3

Pecan Pan Glaze

2/3 cup	butter, melted	150 mL
2/3 cup	packed brown sugar	150 mL
2/3 cup	corn syrup	150 mL
1 cup	chopped pecans	250 mL
1 cup	raisins	250 mL

1. Into a bowl or plastic bag, measure salt, rice flour, potato starch, tapioca starch, xanthan gum, cinnamon and yeast. Mix well and set aside.

2. Into bread machine baking pan, measure water, vinegar, banana, honey and butter; add eggs. Insert pan into the oven chamber. Select **Dough Cycle**. Allow liquids to mix for approximately 2 minutes. Gradually add dry ingredients as bread machine is mixing. Try to incorporate within 1 to 2 minutes. Scrape with rubber spatula while adding dry ingredients. When mixing and kneading are complete, remove the kneading blade.

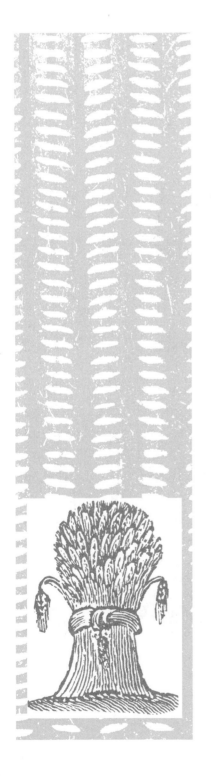

3. Glaze: In a bowl combine butter, brown sugar and corn syrup. Spread half the mixture in each baking pan. Sprinkle each with half the pecans and raisins. Dip rubber spatula and a large spoon in water then drop the soft dough by spoonfuls into the pans. Do not smooth the tops. Cover and let rise in a warm, draft-free place for 40 to 50 minutes or until not quite doubled in volume. Meanwhile, preheat oven to 375° F (190° C).

4. Bake in preheated oven for 35 to 45 minutes or until sticky buns sound hollow when tapped on the top. Immediately invert pan over a serving platter. Allow to stand for 5 minutes before removing pan. Serve warm.

Here's a quartet of unusual ingredients — spelt, amaranth, kamut, quinoa (pronounced "keen-wa"), combined in a light-textured nutritious loaf.

Tip

Purchase grains in small amounts at bulk or health food stores. Store in airtight containers in the refrigerator.

Yes, you're reading it right: The 1.5 lb (750 g) recipe contains *more* yeast than the 2 lb (1 kg).

Variation

Semolina or cornmeal can be substituted for one of the ancient grains.

Ancient Grains Bread

1.5 LB (750 G)

1 1/4 cups	water	300 mL
1/4 cup	nonfat dry milk	50 mL
1 tsp	salt	5 mL
2 tbsp	packed brown sugar	25 mL
2 tbsp	vegetable oil	25 mL
3 cups	bread flour	750 mL
1/2 cup	spelt flour	125 mL
1/4 cup	amaranth flour	50 mL
1/4 cup	kamut flour	50 mL
1/4 cup	quinoa flour	50 mL
1 3/4 tsp	bread machine yeast	8 mL

2 LB (1 KG)

1 1/2 cups	water	375 mL
1/3 cup	nonfat dry milk	75 mL
1 1/2 tsp	salt	7 mL
3 tbsp	packed brown sugar	45 mL
3 tbsp	vegetable oil	45 mL
3 3/4 cups	bread flour	925 mL
1/2 cup	spelt flour	125 mL
1/4 cup	amaranth flour	50 mL
1/4 cup	kamut flour	50 mL
1/4 cup	quinoa flour	50 mL
1 1/2 tsp	bread machine yeast	7 mL

1. Measure ingredients into baking pan in the order recommended by the manufacturer. Insert pan into the oven chamber. Select **Basic Cycle**.

USING THE RAPID ONE- AND TWO-HOUR BASIC CYCLES

Yeast bread normally requires 3 to 4 hours to produce a soft, even-textured loaf. The new "Rapid Cycles" available on many bread machines today allow you to accelerate the process.

Preparing bread in less time means decreasing the kneading and proofing times, as well as increasing the proofing and baking temperatures. As a result, the loaf is shorter and denser. The loaf may have a thicker smoother crust with a lengthwise crack on the top. The texture may be similar to a pound cake — uneven, with some large holes.

For successful rapid baking, follow these helpful suggestions:

- Heat the water to 125° F (55° C).
- Warm the eggs to room temperature by covering with warm (not hot) water for up to 5 minutes.
- Have all remaining ingredients at room temperature.
- As soon as you start the bread machine, scrape the sides and bottom of the bread pan with a rubber or plastic spatula. Continue to scrape until all the dry ingredients are mixed in.
- Slash the top crust once it has started to bake. There should be approximately 40 minutes (display window reads 0:40) left on the program. This allows any one-hour loaf to rise higher, resulting in an improved interior texture and crust.

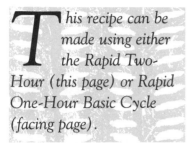

This recipe can be made using either the Rapid Two-Hour (this page) or Rapid One-Hour Basic Cycle (facing page).

Tip

No added fat in this recipe! The ground flaxseed keeps this bread moist.

Other recipes with no added fat include 12-GRAIN ROLLS (see recipe, page 59), SPINACH PITAS (see recipe, page 43) and SOURDOUGH BAGUETTES (see recipe, page 93).

For instructions on grinding flaxseeds, see Techniques Glossary, page 183.

Yes, you're reading it right: The 1.5 lb (750 g) recipe contains the *same* amount of yeast as the 2 lb (1 kg).

Quick Low-Fat Honey Flaxseed Bread

Rapid Two-Hour Basic Recipe

1.5 LB (750 G)

1 1/4 cups	water	300 mL
1/4 cup	nonfat dry milk	50 mL
1 1/4 tsp	salt	6 mL
1/4 cup	honey	50 mL
3 1/4 cups	bread flour	800 mL
3/4 cup	ground flaxseed	175 mL
2 1/4 tsp	bread machine yeast	11 mL

2 LB (1 KG)

1 2/3 cups	water	400 mL
1/3 cup	nonfat dry milk	75 mL
1 1/2 tsp	salt	7 mL
1/4 cup	honey	50 mL
4 cups	bread flour	1000 mL
1 cup	ground flaxseed	250 mL
2 1/4 tsp	bread machine yeast	11 mL

1. Measure ingredients into baking pan in the order recommended by the manufacturer. Insert pan into the oven chamber. Select **Rapid Two-Hour Basic Cycle**.

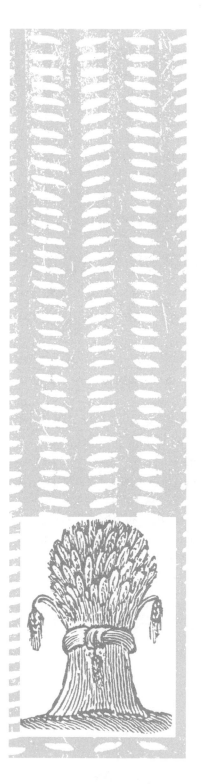

Rapid One-Hour Basic Recipe

1 1/4 cups	water (warmed to 125° F [55° C])	300 mL
1/4 cup	nonfat dry milk	50 mL
1 1/4 tsp	salt	6 mL
1/4 cup	honey	50 mL
3 cups	bread flour	750 mL
1/2 cup	ground flaxseed	125 mL
2 tbsp	bread machine yeast	25 mL

1. Measure ingredients into baking pan in the order recommended by the manufacturer. Insert pan into the oven chamber. Select **Rapid One-Hour Basic Cycle**. When 40 minutes remain on the bread machine display window, take a *lame* or sharp knife and quickly slash the top diagonally.

*E*njoyed by Swiss, Germans and Austrians today, research suggests spelt was a dietary mainstay 9000 years ago. The nutty, whole-grain flavor and wheaty aroma of this bread are a bonus to its high fiber and B-vitamin content.

Tip

Although spelt contains gluten, it is tolerated by many "wheat sensitive" people.

This recipe is based on using light spelt flour. If you want to use the dark variety increase yeast by 1/4 tsp (1 mL). The loaf is shorter and finer textured.

Yes, you're reading it right: The 1.5 lb (750 g) recipe contains *more* yeast than the 2 lb (1 kg).

Variation

For added texture and flavor, add 1/2 cup (125 mL) of flaxseeds or toasted almonds.

Spelt Bread

1.5 LB (750 G)

1/2 cup	water	125 mL
1/2 cup	unsweetened apple juice	125 mL
2	eggs	2
1 1/2 tsp	salt	7 mL
2 tbsp	packed brown sugar	25 mL
2 tbsp	vegetable oil	25 mL
3 1/4 cups	light spelt flour (see Tip, at left)	800 mL
1/3 cup	cornmeal	75 mL
1 1/4 tsp	bread machine yeast	6 mL

2 LB (1 KG)

2/3 cup	water	150 mL
2/3 cup	unsweetened apple juice	150 mL
2	eggs	2
1 3/4 tsp	salt	8 mL
3 tbsp	packed brown sugar	45 mL
3 tbsp	vegetable oil	45 mL
4 1/4 cups	light spelt flour (see Tip, at left)	1050 mL
1/2 cup	cornmeal	125 mL
3/4 tsp	bread machine yeast	4 mL

1. Measure ingredients into baking pan in the order recommended by the manufacturer. Insert pan into the oven chamber. Select **Basic Cycle.**

*P*lenty of fiber and just the right amount of sweetness makes a great combination in this bread.

Tip

Look for a bran cereal that contains at least 10 g fiber per 1/2-cup (125 mL) serving.

Other high-fiber breads include MAPLE BANANA FLAXSEED (see recipe, page 78), ALMOND APRICOT YOGURT (see recipe, page 73) and AMISH SEED BREAD (see recipe, page 74).

High-Fiber Carrot Bran Bread

1.5 LB (750 G)

3/4 cup	water	175 mL
1 cup	grated carrots	250 mL
1 1/4 tsp	salt	6 mL
1 tbsp	packed brown sugar	15 mL
2 tbsp	vegetable oil	25 mL
3/4 cup	whole-wheat flour	175 mL
1 1/2 cups	bread flour	375 mL
1/2 cup	high-fiber bran cereal	125 mL
1/3 cup	buttermilk powder	75 mL
1/2 cup	pitted dates	125 mL
1 3/4 tsp	bread machine yeast	8 mL

2 LB (1 KG)

1 cup	water	250 mL
1 cup	grated carrots	250 mL
1 1/2 tsp	salt	7 mL
2 tbsp	packed brown sugar	25 mL
2 tbsp	vegetable oil	25 mL
1 1/2 cups	whole-wheat flour	300 mL
1 3/4 cups	bread flour	500 mL
1/2 cup	high-fiber bran cereal	125 mL
1/2 cup	buttermilk powder	125 mL
3/4 cup	pitted dates	175 mL
2 tsp	bread machine yeast	10 mL

1. Measure ingredients into baking pan in the order recommended by the manufacturer. Insert pan into the oven chamber. Select **Whole Wheat Cycle**.

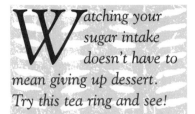

atching your sugar intake doesn't have to mean giving up dessert. Try this tea ring and see!

Tip

For information on sugar substitutes that can hold up to baking temperatures, see Ingredient Glossary, page 177.

Other sugar-free recipes are MOROCCAN ANISE BREAD (see recipe, page 47) and SWISS RYE (see recipe, page 128).

Variation

Substitute applesauce or any other sugar-free fruit spread for the apricot spread.

Sugar-Free Apricot Tea Ring

Makes 2 rings

Baking sheet, lightly greased

Bread

1 cup	milk (room temperature)	250 mL
1/4 cup	unsweetened orange juice	50 mL
1	egg	1
3/4 tsp	salt	4 mL
1/4 cup	granulated sugar substitute (see Tip, at left)	50 mL
2 tbsp	butter	25 mL
4 cups	bread flour	1000 mL
1 1/4 tsp	bread machine yeast	6 mL

Apricot Filling

1/4 to 1/2 cup	dried apricots (optional)	50 to 125 mL
1/3 to 2/3 cup	sugar-free apricot spread	75 to 150 mL

Almond Topping

2 tbsp	milk	25 mL
2 tbsp	granulated sugar substitute (see Tip, at left)	25 mL
1/2 cup	sliced almonds	125 mL

1. Measure ingredients into baking pan in the order recommended by the manufacturer. Insert pan into the oven chamber. Select **Dough Cycle**. Remove dough to a lightly floured surface. Cover with a large bowl and let rest for 10 to 15 minutes.

2. Filling: In a bowl snip apricots into 6 pieces. Add apricot spread and mix gently; set aside.

Recipe continues…

SOUP-IN-A-BREAD-BOWL (PAGE 142) ➤

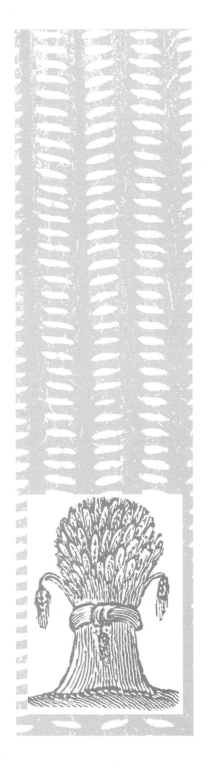

3. Divide dough in half. Roll out each half to a 12- by 6-inch (30 by 15 cm) rectangle. Spread each with one-half the filling to within 1/2 inch (1 cm) of the edges. Beginning at the long side, roll jellyroll style. Pinch to seal seam. Form into a ring, pinching ends together. Place on prepared baking sheet. With scissors, make cuts two-thirds of the way through the ring, 1 inch (2.5 cm) apart. Repeat with remaining half of dough. Cover and let rise in a warm, draft-free place for 30 to 45 minutes or until doubled in volume. Meanwhile, preheat oven to 350° F (180° C).

4. Brush risen dough with milk. Sprinkle with sugar substitute and sliced almonds. Bake in preheated oven for 20 to 25 minutes or until tea rings sound hollow when tapped on the bottom.

◄ LEMON CAKE (PAGE 170)

W*ith its dark gold, shiny crust studded with seeds, this loaf is so attractive, you'll forget it's healthy too.*

Tip

Because soy flour contains no gluten at all, you can't use too much in yeast breads.

Yes, you're reading it right: The 1.5 lb (750 g) recipe contains the *same* amount of yeast as the 2 lb (1 kg).

Variation

Substitute any gluten-free flour for the soy flour.

Seed-and-Soy Loaf

1.5 LB (750 G)

1 1/4 cups	water	300 mL
1/4 cup	nonfat dry milk	50 mL
1 1/2 tsp	salt	7 mL
2 tbsp	honey	25 mL
1 tbsp	molasses	15 mL
2 tbsp	vegetable oil	25 mL
1 1/4 cups	whole-wheat flour	300 mL
1 3/4 cups	bread flour	425 mL
1/2 cup	soy flour	125 mL
1/4 cup	sesame seeds	50 mL
1/4 cup	sunflower seeds	50 mL
1 tbsp	caraway seeds	15 mL
1 1/2 tsp	bread machine yeast	7 mL

2 LB (1 KG)

1 1/2 cups	water	375 mL
1/3 cup	nonfat dry milk	75 mL
1 3/4 tsp	salt	8 mL
3 tbsp	honey	45 mL
2 tbsp	molasses	25 mL
2 tbsp	vegetable oil	25 mL
1 1/2 cups	whole-wheat flour	325 mL
2 1/4 cups	bread flour	575 mL
3/4 cup	soy flour	175 mL
1/3 cup	sesame seeds	75 mL
1/3 cup	sunflower seeds	75 mL
1 tbsp	caraway seeds	15 mL
1 1/2 tsp	bread machine yeast	7 mL

1. Measure ingredients into baking pan in the order recommended by the manufacturer. Insert pan into the oven chamber. Select **Whole Wheat Cycle**.

BEYOND BREADS

TIPS FOR MAKING PERFECT PASTA	164
BASIC FRESH PASTA (SPAGHETTI)	165
FRESH SPINACH PASTA (FETTUCCINE)	166
FRESH TOMATO-HERB PASTA	167
TIPS FOR MAKING CAKES AND COOKIES IN YOUR BREAD MACHINE	168
BANANA QUICK BREAD	169
LEMON CAKE	170
PINEAPPLE COCONUT CAKE	171
OATMEAL RAISIN BARS	172
RASPBERRY CHEESECAKE	173
TIPS FOR MAKING JAMS AND JELLIES	174
APPLE JELLY	174
STRAWBERRY RHUBARB JAM	175

As you might expect, a bread machine is wonderful for baking breads and loaves. But it can do so much more — like make fresh pasta, cakes and cookies, even jams and jellies. Try these recipes and discover all the possibilities for yourself.

TIPS FOR MAKING PERFECT PASTA

- Depending on the bread machine you use, some recipes for pasta dough in this chapter may be a little too dry. In such cases, try adding 1 to 2 tsp (5 to 10 mL) extra water.

- Some bread machines can produce smooth, workable dough in a single **Pasta Cycle**, while others require 2 or 3 cycles. Repeat cycle as often as necessary to ensure all dry ingredients are incorporated.

- When using **Dough Cycle**, allow bread machine to knead just as long as necessary to ensure all dry ingredients are incorporated.

- Rolling and cutting the dough is much easier with a pasta machine — and the instructions in our recipes assume you will be using one. If you don't have a pasta machine, however, you can make do with a rolling pin and a sharp knife.

- Keep pasta dough in a plastic bag until it is rolled and cut. It loses moisture and dries out quickly, making it difficult to work through the pasta machine.

- Roll pasta dough to a thickness of 1/16 to 1/8 inch (1 to 2 mm). Thicker pasta dough is easier to work with.

- When using a pasta machine, work with only a small amount of dough at a time. Continue to feed through the smooth rollers of the pasta machine until dough is smooth, shiny and pliable. Depending on the consistency of the pasta dough produced by your bread machine, this may require 8 (or more) repetitions.

- Cook fresh pasta in a large amount of boiling water only until it is *al dente* (tender but firm). Cooking will take longer for thicker pasta.

- If not serving immediately, rinse cooked pasta under cold water to stop further cooking. Drain and refrigerate for up to 3 days or freeze for up to 1 month.

*L*et your bread machine do the work of making the pasta dough while you (or your family or friends) roll and cut the pasta into spaghetti — or any other pasta shape you wish.

Tip

A pasta machine is invaluable for making straight, uniformly shaped pasta. But if you don't have one, you can always use a rolling pin and a sharp knife.

Store fresh cooked pasta in the refrigerator for up to 3 days. Reheat pasta in boiling water for 1 to 2 minutes, being careful not to overcook it.

Variation

Substitute pasta flour for the semolina flour.

Try using a flavored olive oil instead of the plain variety.

Basic Fresh Pasta (Spaghetti)

2/3 cup	water	150 mL
1	egg	1
2 tbsp	olive oil	25 mL
1 tsp	salt	5 mL
2 1/2 cups	semolina flour	625 mL

1. Measure ingredients into baking pan in the order recommended by the manufacturer. Insert pan into the oven chamber. Select **Pasta** or **Dough Cycle**.

2. With a rubber spatula, scrape down sides of baking pan and kneading blade. Remove dough to a lightly floured surface. Divide dough into 4 to 6 portions; place in a plastic bag to prevent drying. Position the rollers of pasta machine at the widest point. Using one portion at a time, roll the dough, then fold it either lengthwise or crosswise. Continue rolling and folding dough until smooth, shiny and elastic. If dough is sticky, dust with flour.

3. Begin to roll dough thinner by positioning the rollers closer and closer together. Continue until the pasta is between 1/8 to 1/4 inch (2 and 5 mm) thick. Replace the smooth roller with a spaghetti cutter and cut dough to desired length and width. Cook in a large pot of boiling salted water for 3 to 5 minutes or until *al dente*.

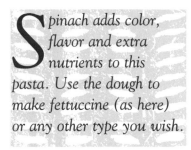

Spinach adds color, flavor and extra nutrients to this pasta. Use the dough to make fettuccine (as here) or any other type you wish.

Tip

Fresh pasta cooks much faster than dried pasta. If you're not careful, it will turn from *al dente* to *mush* before you know it.

A pasta machine is invaluable for making straight, uniformly shaped pasta. But if you don't have one, you can always use a rolling pin and a sharp knife.

Variation

Use fresh or frozen cooked spinach for this recipe; just be sure it is well drained.

Fresh Spinach Pasta (Fettuccine)

1/3 cup	water	75 mL
2	eggs	2
1/4 cup	finely chopped drained cooked spinach	50 mL
2 tbsp	olive oil	25 mL
1/2 tsp	salt	2 mL
2 3/4 cups	semolina flour	675 mL

1. Measure ingredients into baking pan in the order recommended by the manufacturer. Insert pan into the oven chamber. Select **Pasta** or **Dough Cycle**.

2. With a rubber spatula, scrape down sides of baking pan and kneading blade. Remove dough to a lightly floured surface. Divide dough into 4 to 6 portions; place in a plastic bag to prevent drying. Position the rollers of pasta machine at the widest point. Using one portion at a time, roll the dough, then fold it either lengthwise or crosswise. Continue rolling and folding dough until smooth, shiny and elastic. If dough is sticky, dust with flour.

3. Begin to roll thinner by positioning the rollers closer and closer together. Continue until the pasta is between 1/8 and 1/4 inch (2 and 5 mm) thick. Replace smooth roller with a fettuccine cutter and cut dough to desired length and width. Cook in a large amount of boiling salted water for 3 to 5 minutes or until *al dente*.

ere's pasta with the flavor of Italian tomato sauce built right in!

Tip

Use dry (not oil-packed) sun-dried tomatoes.

A pasta machine is invaluable for making straight, uniformly shaped pasta. But if you don't have one, you can always use a rolling pin and a sharp knife.

Fresh Tomato-Herb Pasta

1/3 cup	water	75 mL
2	eggs	2
3 tbsp	tomato paste	45 mL
1/4 cup	finely snipped sun-dried tomatoes	50 mL
2 tbsp	olive oil	25 mL
1/2 tsp	salt	2 mL
2 3/4 cups	semolina flour	675 mL
3 tbsp	packed snipped fresh basil leaves	45 mL

1. Measure ingredients into baking pan in the order recommended by the manufacturer. Insert pan into the oven chamber. Select **Pasta** or **Dough Cycle**.

2. With a rubber spatula, scrape down sides of baking pan and kneading blade. Remove dough to a lightly floured surface. Divide dough into 4 to 6 portions; place in a plastic bag to prevent drying. Position the rollers of pasta machine at the widest point. Using one portion at a time, roll the dough, then fold it either lengthwise or crosswise. Continue rolling and folding dough until smooth, shiny and elastic. If dough is sticky, dust with flour.

3. Begin to roll thinner by positioning the rollers closer and closer together. Continue until the pasta is between 1/8 and 1/4 inch (2 and 5 mm) thick. Replace smooth roller with a cutter and cut dough to length and width desired. Cook in a large amount of boiling salted water for 3 to 5 minutes or until *al dente*.

TIPS FOR BAKING CAKES AND COOKIES IN YOUR BREAD MACHINE

- Before attempting these recipes, read your bread machine manual for any information about making cakes and cookies. Follow any instructions carefully.

- Add the ingredients in the order recommended in the recipe.

- Cut soft shortening, cream cheese and butter into 1-inch (2.5 cm) cubes before adding.

- All ingredients should be at room temperature or warmed according to the recipe instructions. Refrigerated eggs can be warmed in the shell by placing them in a bowl of hot (but not boiling) water for 5 minutes.

- To ensure even mixing, scrape the corners, sides and bottom of the baking pan with a rubber or plastic spatula to incorporate all dry ingredients.

- In order to bake completely, some cakes must be left in the bread machine baking pan, using the **Keep Warm Cycle** or **Bake Cycle**. The cake is done when a long wooden skewer inserted into the center of the cake comes out clean.

- Cool cakes in baking pan for 10 minutes, then turn out onto a wire rack to cool completely.

- If using your bread machine to bake a commercially pre-pared cake mix, choose the large 15 to 18 oz (400 to 550 g) size. The "pudding-in-the-mix" type works best.

*F*ast and easy to prepare, this bread makes a great snack for the family or a nice housewarming gift for a new neighbor.

Tip

Test for doneness by inserting a long wooden skewer into the center of the quick bread. If it comes out clean, the bread is fully baked.

For a moist "quick-bread" texture, cool overnight before slicing.

Some bread machines may require up to 50 minutes on the **Keep Warm Cycle** before the quick bread is baked. For specifications on the length of this cycle, and for information on how to use it, check the user's manual for your bread machine.

Banana Quick Bread

Makes 1 loaf

1/2 cup	milk (room temperature)	125 mL
1 cup	mashed ripe bananas	250 mL
2	eggs	2
1/2 tsp	salt	2 mL
1 cup	granulated sugar	250 mL
1/2 cup	vegetable oil	125 mL
2 1/4 cups	all-purpose flour	550 mL
2 tsp	baking powder	10 mL
1 tsp	baking soda	5 mL
1/2 cup	chopped walnuts	125 mL

1. Measure ingredients into baking pan in the order recommended by the manufacturer. Insert pan into the oven chamber. Select **Cake Cycle**.

2. Halfway through mixing time, using a rubber spatula, scrape down sides of baking pan and the kneading blade. When signal sounds indicating the end of cycle, test for doneness with a wooden skewer. If ready, remove baking pan from bread machine. If not, keep in bread machine on **Keep Warm Cycle** for 10 to 30 minutes or on **Bake Cycle** until baked.

3. Sit baking pan on a cooling rack for 10 minutes. Turn cake out onto a serving plate and set aside to cool completely.

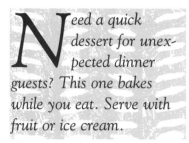

eed a quick dessert for unexpected dinner guests? This one bakes while you eat. Serve with fruit or ice cream.

Tip

Using a cake mix may seem like "cheating" — but with all the fresh lemon flavor in this recipe, no one will ever know your secret! We always keep a cake mix in the cupboard for emergencies.

Variation

For an orange version of this cake, substitute orange juice and zest for the lemon, both in the cake and the syrup.

Lemon Cake

Makes 1 cake

	Cake	
1	pkg (18 oz [510 g]) yellow, golden or lemon pudding cake mix	1
1 cup	water	250 mL
3	eggs	3
1/3 cup	vegetable oil	75 mL
1 tbsp	fresh lemon juice	15 mL
2 tsp	grated lemon zest	10 mL

	Lemon Syrup	
1/2 cup	granulated sugar	125 mL
3 tbsp	fresh lemon juice	45 mL

1. Measure cake ingredients into baking pan in the order recommended by the manufacturer. Insert pan into the oven chamber. Select **Cake Cycle**.

2. Halfway through mixing time, using a rubber spatula, scrape down sides of baking pan and kneading blade. When signal sounds indicating the end of cycle, test for doneness with a wooden skewer. If ready, remove baking pan from bread machine. If not, keep in bread machine on **Keep Warm Cycle** for 10 to 30 minutes or on **Bake Cycle** until baked.

3. Lemon syrup: In a small saucepan over low heat, combine sugar and lemon juice. Heat, stirring constantly, until sugar is dissolved. With a long wooden skewer, poke several holes through the cake as soon as it is removed from the bread machine. Spoon warm syrup over the hot cake. Sit baking pan on a cooling rack for 30 minutes. Turn cake out onto a serving plate and set aside to cool completely.

Here's a delicious made-from-scratch cake prepared in the bread machine. It's quick and easy — and there's only one pan to wash!

Tip

Test for doneness by inserting a long wooden skewer into the center of the cake. If it comes out clean, the cake is fully baked.

Variation

For a different texture, replace flaked coconut with shredded or desiccated coconut.

Add 1/2 cup (125 mL) chopped pecans.

Pineapple Coconut Cake

Makes 1 cake

1 cup	granulated sugar	250 mL
1/2 cup	shortening	125 mL
2	eggs, slightly beaten	2
3/4 tsp	orange extract	4 mL
1	can (8 oz [227 mL]) crushed pineapple, with juice	1
1 tsp	salt	5 mL
2 1/2 cups	all-purpose flour	625 mL
4 tsp	baking powder	20 mL
3/4 cup	unsweetened flaked coconut	175 mL
2 tsp	grated orange zest	10 mL

1. Measure sugar and shortening into baking pan. Add eggs. Insert pan into the oven chamber. Select **Cake Cycle**.

2. Two minutes into mixing time, using a rubber spatula, scrape down sides of baking pan and kneading blade. Stop bread machine after 5 minutes of mixing. Remove baking pan from machine. Add orange extract, pineapple (with juice), salt, flour, baking powder, coconut and zest. Insert pan into the oven chamber. Select **Cake Cycle**.

3. Halfway through mixing time, using a rubber spatula, scrape down sides of baking pan and kneading blade. When signal sounds indicating the end of cycle, test for doneness with a wooden skewer. If ready, remove baking pan from bread machine. If not, keep in bread machine on **Keep Warm Cycle** for 10 to 30 minutes or on **Bake Cycle** until baked. Sit baking pan on a cooling rack for 10 minutes. Turn cake out onto a serving plate and set aside to cool completely.

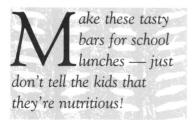

*M*ake these tasty
bars for school
lunches — just
*don't tell the kids that
they're nutritious!*

Tip

To blend all the ingredients thoroughly, thick cookie doughs may need to be processed through the **Mixing Cycle** 2 or 3 times.

If your bread machine doesn't have a **Mixing Cycle**, use the **Dough Cycle**; keep an eye on the dough and stop cycle when mixing is complete.

Variation

Oatmeal Raisin Cookies: Drop prepared dough, by the spoonful, onto a lightly greased baking sheet. Bake in preheated oven for 10 to 12 minutes or until baked. Remove from baking sheet and cool on a rack.

Oatmeal Raisin Bars

Makes 16 bars

9-inch (3 L) square pan, lightly greased

1/3 cup	melted butter	75 mL
2/3 cup	packed brown sugar	150 mL
2	eggs	2
1 tsp	vanilla	5 mL
1 tsp	salt	5 mL
1 cup	all-purpose flour	250 mL
2 cups	quick-cooking oats	500 mL
1 tsp	baking powder	5 mL
1 1/2 cups	raisins	375 mL

1. Measure ingredients into baking pan in the order recommended by the manufacturer. Insert pan into the oven chamber. Select **Mixing Cycle**.

2. Halfway through mixing time, using a rubber spatula, scrape down sides of baking pan and kneading blade. (If ingredients are not well mixed, restart the **Mixing Cycle**.) Meanwhile, preheat oven to 350° F (180° C).

3. When signal sounds indicating the end of cycle, remove baking pan from bread machine. Press dough into prepared pan. Bake in preheated oven for 30 to 35 minutes.

Can you really make cheesecake in a bread machine? Absolutely! And here's the recipe that proves it.

Tip

Check the manufacturer's instructions for the length of the **Kneading Cycle**. It should be approximately 7 to 8 minutes.

To prevent lumps from forming, soften cream cheese completely before adding to the pan.

To warm eggs, place in a bowl of hot (not boiling) water for 5 minutes.

Variation

Use any fruit-flavored yogurt and a matching fruit topping.

Raspberry Cheesecake

Makes 1 cake

1 cup	granulated sugar	250 mL
2	pkgs (each 8 oz [250 g]) cream cheese (room temperature)	2
4	eggs, warmed (see Tip, at left)	4
3/4 cup	raspberry-flavored yogurt	175 mL
1/2 tsp	lemon juice	2 mL
1/8 tsp	salt	0.5 mL
2 tbsp	all-purpose flour	25 mL
1	pkg (10 oz [300 g]) frozen sweetened raspberries, thawed	1

1. Measure sugar and cream cheese into baking pan. Insert pan into the oven chamber. Select **Cake Cycle**. (If available, select the 1.5 lb (750 g) loaf size with a light crust setting.) One minute before the mixing ends, press Stop. With a rubber spatula, scrape sides of baking pan and kneading blade.

2. Add eggs, yogurt, lemon juice, salt and flour. Select **Cake Cycle**. (If desired, remove the kneading blade after the kneading is complete but before the cheesecake begins to bake; this eliminates the kneading blade-sized hole in the cheesecake.) When signal sounds indicating end of cycle, test for doneness. A stainless steel knife inserted in the middle should come out clean. If not completely baked, keep in bread machine on **Keep Warm Cycle** for 10 to 30 minutes or on **Bake Cycle** until baked.

3. Sit baking pan on a cooling rack for 10 minutes. Carefully turn cheesecake out onto a serving plate and set aside to cool completely, then refrigerate.

4. To serve: In a food processor or blender, purée thawed raspberries. Press through a fine sieve. Spoon purée onto individual serving plates. Top with cheesecake.

TIPS FOR MAKING JAMS AND JELLIES

- Before attempting these recipes, read your bread machine manual for any information about making jams and jellies. Follow any instructions carefully.

- To prevent jam from boiling over, don't exceed quantities given in recipes.

- Use oven mitts when handling hot jam — it's hotter than fat used in deep frying!

- Pour jam into sterilized jars. Store in the refrigerator for 3 to 4 weeks. Don't forget to date the product.

You don't need seasonal fruit to make this jelly — it's easy to prepare all year round.

Tip

Jelly will appear very thin at first. But don't worry — it will thicken as it cools in the refrigerator.

Variation

Substitute white grape juice or any other type of unsweetened fruit juice for the apple juice.

Apple Jelly

3 cups	unsweetened apple juice	750 mL
1 cup	granulated sugar	250 mL
2 tbsp	unflavored gelatin	25 mL
1 tbsp	lemon juice	15 mL

1. Measure ingredients into baking pan in the order recommended by the manufacturer. Insert pan into the oven chamber. Select **Jam Cycle**.

2. When cycle is complete, wait for 15 minutes before opening lid or removing baking pan. Wearing oven mitts, carefully remove the baking pan from the bread machine. Cool in pan for at least 30 minutes.

3. Pour jelly into sterilized jars and seal. Refrigerate to thicken. Jelly will keep in the refrigerator for up to 4 weeks.

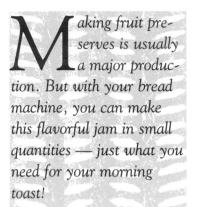

Making fruit preserves is usually a major production. But with your bread machine, you can make this flavorful jam in small quantities — just what you need for your morning toast!

Tip

For the smoothest texture, use thin, tender stalks of rhubarb.

Variation

Leave the strawberries whole for a chunky type of jam. For a more jelly-like consistency, chop the fruit into smaller pieces.

Strawberry Rhubarb Jam

3 cups	fresh rhubarb, cut into 1/2-inch (1 cm) pieces	750 mL
3 cups	hulled fresh strawberries	750 mL
2 1/2 cups	granulated sugar	625 mL

1. Measure ingredients into baking pan in the order recommended by the manufacturer. Insert pan into the oven chamber. Select **Jam Cycle**.

2. When cycle is complete, wait 15 minutes before opening lid or removing baking pan. Wearing oven mitts, carefully remove the baking pan from the bread machine. Cool in pan for at least 30 minutes.

3. Pour jam into sterilized jars and seal. Refrigerate for up to 4 weeks.

Equipment Glossary

Baguette pan. A metal baking pan, divided into two sections shaped like long thin loaves. The bottom surface may be perforated with small holes to produce a crisp crust and reduce the baking time.

Baking liners. Reusable sheets of nonstick coated fiberglass. Flexible and food-safe, they are used to eliminate the need to grease and flour. Wash, rinse well and dry before storing.

Baking stone. Available in different sizes and shapes, baking stones are made of unglazed quarry or ceramic tile (the same material used to line brick ovens.) Use for pitas, pizza and focaccia when a crisp crust is desired. *To use a baking stone:* Preheat on bottom rack of oven for at least 15 to 20 minutes before using. *To clean:* Cool completely, scrape off any burnt matter, then wipe stone with a damp cloth.

Banneton. A woven basket used for rising bread dough. Dust well with flour before using. The crust will have the pattern of the basket after baking.

Clay bakers. These are available in a wide variety of shapes, ranging from loaf pans to bundt pans to flower pots. Before using, grease inside completely. While designed to withstand oven temperatures, they are fragile.

Dough scraper. A rectangular-shaped piece of metal or plastic, with or without a handle, used to lift or cut dough or to scrape and clean a work surface.

Lame. A tool that features an extra-sharp curved blade used by French bakers to make perfectly shaped slashes on risen dough before baking. This ensures the loaf expands to the right shape as it bakes.

Pastry brush. Small brush of nylon or natural bristles used to apply glazes or egg washes to the dough. Thoroughly wash after each use. To store, lay flat or hang on a hook through a hole in the handle.

Pastry wheel. A small, sharp-edged wheel anchored to a handle. The edge of the wheel may be plain or serrated, and is used for marking and cutting pastry dough.

Peel. Not the outside layer of a fruit or vegetable — but a long-handled flat blade, made of wood or metal, used to move pizza or yeast breads on and off baking stones or baking sheets. This prevents the dough from wrinkling as it slides into the oven and protects the baker from burns. *To use a peel:* Generously flour the peel. Slide it under the risen dough or crust and ease it onto the baking stone or oven rack.

Pizza wheel. A large, sharp-edged wheel (without serrations) anchored to a handle. Use it to cut dough for breadsticks, rolls or toasties.

Skewer. A long, thin stick (made of wood or metal) used in baking to test for doneness.

Spatula. A utensil with a handle and blade that can be long or short, narrow or wide, flexible or inflexible. It is used to spread, lift, turn, mix or smooth foods. Spatulas are made of wood, metal, rubber or plastic.

Thermometer. Bakers use this metal-stemmed instrument to test the internal temperature of bread. Stem must be inserted at least 2 inches (5 cm) into the bread for an accurate reading. When bread is baked, it should register 190° F (95° C).

Zester. A tool used to cut very thin strips of outer peel from citrus fruits. It has a short, flat blade tipped with five small holes with sharp edges.

Ingredient Glossary

Almond. Crack open the shell of an almond and you'll find an ivory-colored nut encased in a thin brown skin. With the skin removed, (for technique, see first entry on page 183), the almond is "blanched." In this form, almonds are sold whole, sliced, slivered and ground. Two cups (500 mL) almonds weigh about 12 oz (375 g).

Almond paste. Made of ground blanched almonds, sugar and egg whites, almond paste is coarser, darker and less sweet than **Marzipan** (see page 180). Do not substitute one for the other.

Amaranth. Native to Mexico, this purple-leaved plant produces seeds that are used as a cereal or ground into flour, which is low in gluten.

Anise seeds/star anise. These tiny gray-green, egg-shaped seeds have a distinctive licorice flavor. Anise can also be purchased as a finely ground powder. For recipes that call for anise seeds, half the amount of anise powder can be substituted.

Asiago cheese. A pungent grayish-white hard cheese from northern Italy. Cured for more than 6 months, it's texture is ideal for grating.

Baba. A Polish Easter cake that is traditionally baked in a cylindrical mold. It contains currants and raisins soaked in rum or Kirsch. The same dough is used to make Savarin, a larger variation of Baba. Also known as Baba au Rhum.

Babka. A Polish sweet bread similar to coffee cake, made with rum, almonds, raisins and orange peel.

Barley. A cereal grain with a slightly sweet, nutty, earthy flavor and a chewy texture, sometimes ground into a **flour** with low gluten content. Barley in baked products adds to the starch and soluble fiber content. Barley **flakes** are made from the barley grain and look very similar to rolled oats.

Bell peppers. The sweet-flavored members of the capsicum family (which include chilies and other hot peppers), these peppers have a hollow interior lined with white ribs and seeds attached at the stem end. They are most commonly green, red or yellow, but can also be white or purple.

Brown sugar. A refined sugar with a coating of molasses. It can be purchased coarse or fine and comes in 3 varieties: dark, golden and light.

Buckwheat. Not related, despite its name, to wheat (which is a grain), buckwheat is the seed of a plant from the rhubarb family. Buckwheat flour is dark and strongly flavored. Roasted whole buckwheat, called Kasha, has a strong nutty flavor and chewy texture.

Bulgur. Whole-wheat kernels, with the bran layer removed, that have been cooked, dried and cracked into fragments. In bread recipes, it provides a nutty texture and flavor, as well as a somewhat coarse texture. Cracked wheat can be substituted for bulgur.

Butter. A spread produced from dairy fat and milk solids, butter can be used interchangeably in bread recipes for shortening, oil or margarine.

Buttermilk powder. A dry powder, low in calories, which softens the texture of bread and heightens the flavor of ingredients such as chocolate. It is readily available from bulk- or health-food stores. Keep in an airtight container, since it lumps easily. To substitute for 1 cup (250 mL) fresh buttermilk, use 1 cup (250 mL) water and 1/3 cup (75 mL) buttermilk powder.

Caraway seeds. Small, crescent-shaped seeds of the caraway plant. They have a nutty, peppery, licorice-like flavor.

Cardamom. This popular spice is a member of the ginger family. A long green or brown pod contains the strong, spicy, lemon-flavored seed. It is used in Middle Eastern, Indian and Scandinavian cooking.

Cereal. Any grain that yields an edible part such as wheat, oats, rye, rice or corn.

Cereal, 3-grain. See Red River cereal.

Cereal, 7-grain. Contains barley flakes, triticale flour, corn flakes, steel-cut oats, rye meal, cracked wheat, flax seed and hulled millet. And yes, for anyone who's counting, there are 8 ingredients, not 7!

Cereal, 12-grain. Contains triticale, steel-cut oats, barley flakes, sesame, buckwheat, rye meal, oats, corn, cracked wheat, millet, flax and sunflower seeds. *Note:* All multi-grain cereals can be used interchangeably in bread machine recipes.

Cheddar cheese. Always select an aged, good-quality Cheddar for bread machine recipes. (The flavor of mild or medium Cheddar is not strong enough for bread machine baking.) Weight/volume equivalents are:
4 oz (120 g) = 1 cup (250 mL) grated;
2 oz (60 g) = 1/2 cup (125 mL) grated;
1 1/2 oz (45 g) = 1/3 cup (75 mL) grated.

Coffee cake. A sweet dough made with yeast which produces a texture more like cake than bread.

Cornmeal. The dried, ground kernels of white, yellow or blue corn. It has a gritty texture and is available in coarse, medium and fine grind. Its starchy-sweet flavor is most commonly associated with cornbread – a regional specialty of the Southern United States.

Corn syrup. A thick, sweet syrup made from cornstarch, sold as clear (light) or brown (dark) varieties. The latter has caramel flavor and color added.

Cracked wheat. Similar to bulgur, for which it can be substituted in bread recipes, except that it is not pre-cooked and has not had the bran removed.

Cranberry. Grown in bogs on low vines, these sweet-tart berries are available fresh, frozen and dried. Fresh cranberries are available only in season — typically from mid-October until January, depending on your location — but can be frozen right in the bag. Substitute dried cranberries for sour cherries, raisins or currants.

Currant. Similar in appearance to small, dark raisins, currants are made by drying a special seedless variety of grape. Not the same as a type of berry that goes by the same name.

Dates. The fruit of the date palm tree, dates are long and oval in shape, with a paper-thin skin that turns from green to dark brown when ripe. Eaten fresh or dried, dates have a very sweet, light-brown flesh around a long, narrow seed.

Dough enhancer. Any of several compounds that can be added to dough to increase its strength and tolerance, extend shelf life and make a lighter-textured bread. Examples of dough enhancers include tofu and vitamin C.

Eggplant. Ranging in color and shape from dark purple and pear-like to light mauve and cylindrical, eggplant has a light, spongy flesh that, while bland on its own, is remarkable for its ability to absorb other flavors in cooking.

Fennel seeds. Small, oval, green-brown seeds with prominent ridges and a mild anise (licorice-like) flavor and aroma. Available whole or ground, they are used in Italian and Central European cookery, particularly in rye or pumpernickel breads.

Feta cheese. A crumbly, white, Greek-style cheese, with a salty, tangy flavor. Store in the refrigerator, in its brine, and drain well before using.

Fig. A pear-shaped fruit with a thick, soft skin. Eaten fresh or dried, the tan-colored sweet flesh contains many tiny edible seeds.

Filbert. See Hazelnut.

Flaxseed. Thin and oval shaped, dark brown in color, flaxseeds add a crunchy texture to breads. Research indicates that flaxseed can aid in lowering blood cholesterol levels. Ground flaxseed (also known as Linseed) go stale quickly, so purchase only the amount needed; store in the refrigerator.

Garlic. An edible bulb composed of several sections (cloves), each covered with a papery skin. An essential ingredient in many styles of cooking.

Ginger. While fresh ginger root is used most often in savory dishes, the dried, ground form is favored in baking.

Gluten. A natural protein in wheat flour that becomes elastic with the addition of moisture and kneading. Gluten traps gases produced by yeast inside the dough and causes it to rise. The stronger the gluten, the greater the loaf volume. Gluten also aids the dough in supporting added ingredients, such as grains, nuts and dried fruit.

Gluten flour. When the gluten content of flour exceeds 80% gluten, it is called gluten flour (or "vital wheat gluten" or just "gluten"). It may be purchased from bulk food stores and added to breads with low-gluten flours to provide extra height.

Golden raisins. See Raisins.

Granola. A mixture of dried fruit, grains and nuts. Available in sweetened or unsweetened varieties, it is often used as an ingredient in hearty breads, or can be eaten alone as a breakfast cereal or snack.

Granulated sugar. A refined, crystalline, white, form of sugar that is also commonly referred to as "table sugar" or just "sugar."

Hazelnut. Also known as filberts, hazelnuts have a rich, sweet, flavor that complements ingredients such as coffee and chocolate. Remove the bitter brown skin before using.

Hazelnut liqueur. Best known as Frangelico, a hazelnut-flavored liqueur made in Italy.

Herbs. Plants whose stems, leaves or flowers are used as a flavoring, either dried or fresh. (*See also* individual herbs.) To substitute fresh herbs for dried, a good rule of thumb is to use three times the amount of fresh as dried. Taste and adjust the amount to suit your preference.

Honey. Sweeter than sugar, honey is available in liquid, honeycomb and creamed varieties. Use liquid honey for bread machine recipes.

Jule Kaga or **Julekage.** A Swedish Christmas bread with candied fruits and cardamom flavor.

Kamut. A large-kerneled, high-protein variety of wheat that was used in ancient times for bread. (Its name is the ancient Egyptian word for wheat.) It has a distinctively nutty taste and contains more nutrients than most types of wheat.

Kasha. See Buckwheat.

Kolachy or **Kolaches.** A Christmas breakfast tradition in Eastern European homes, (particularly those of Czechs and Poles), these sweet buns are typically filled with poppy seeds, nuts, mashed fruit or jam.

Kringle. A Swedish Christmas bread.

Linseed. See Flaxseed (ground).

Malt powder. The dried form of malt syrup (although not interchangeable with it), malt powder provides a distinctive flavor, texture and crust color to breads, and also helps the loaf stay fresh longer. It absorbs moisture and becomes lumpy very quickly, so store in an airtight container. Diastolic malt powder is a highly concentrated form of malt powder and can be substituted using much smaller quantities.

Malt syrup. A byproduct of the process by which barley is soaked, sprouted and dried. The syrup is obtained from the barley by extraction and evaporation of worts — a substance also used to produce beer and certain distilled spirits.

Maple syrup. A very sweet, slightly thick brown liquid made by boiling the sap from North American maple trees.

Margarine. A solid fat derived from one or more types of vegetable oil. Do not use low-fat margarines in bread machine baking, since they contain too much added water.

Marzipan. A sweet paste made from ground almonds, sugar and egg whites. Used as candy filling and for cake decorations, it is sweeter and lighter in color than Almond Paste (see page 177).

Mixed glazed fruit. A mixture of dried candied orange and lemon peel, citron and glazed cherries. Citron, which can be expensive, is often replaced in the mix by candied rutabaga.

Molasses. A byproduct of refining sugar, molasses is a sweet, thick, dark-brown (almost black) liquid. It has a distinctive, slightly bitter flavor and is available in fancy and blackstrap varieties. Use the fancy variety for breads. Store in the refrigerator if used infrequently.

Muesli. A cereal blend of oats, dates, sultanas, oat bran, currants, almonds, sesame seeds, walnuts, pecans, dried apples, wheat germ, flaxseeds and corn grits. It has a relatively high fat content, so should be stored in an airtight container in the refrigerator or freezer to prevent it from becoming rancid.

Oat bran. The outer layer of oat grain. It has a high soluble fiber content, which can help to lower blood cholesterol.

Oats. Confusing in its many variations, the term "oats" generally refers to the cereal grass of the oat grain. When the oat husk has been removed, it is called a *groat*. Oats are steamed and rolled into flat flakes called *rolled oats* or *old-fashioned oats*. When coarsely ground oats are cooked and used for baking, it becomes *oatmeal*. *"Instant"* oats are partially cooked and dried before rolling. They are rolled thinner, cut finer, and may have flavoring ingredients added. They are not recommended for use in bread machines. *"Quick-cooking"* oats are rolled oats that are cut into smaller pieces to reduce the cooking time. For a traditional oat bread texture, use small- or medium-flake oatmeal, but not the "instant cooking" type.

Olives (Kalamata). A large, flavorful variety of Greek olive, typically dark purple in color, and pointed at one end. They are usually sold packed in olive oil or vinegar.

Olive oil. Produced from pressing tree-ripened olives. *Extra virgin* oil is taken from the first cold pressing; it is the finest and fruitiest, pale straw to pale green in color with the least amount of acid, usually less than 1%. *Virgin* oil is taken from a subsequent pressing; it contains 2% acid and is pale yellow. *Light* oil comes from the last pressing; it has a mild flavor, light color and up to 3% acid. It also has a higher smoke point. Product sold as "pure olive oil" has been cleaned and filtered; it is very mild-flavored and has up to 3% acid.

Parsley. A biennial herb with dark green, curly or flat leaves used fresh as a flavoring or garnish. It is also used dried in soups and other mixes. Substitute parsley for half the amount of a strong-flavored herb such as basil.

Pecan. The nut of the hickory tree, pecans have a reddish, mahogany shell and beige flesh. They have a high fat content and are a milder-flavored alternative to walnuts.

Peel (mixed, candied or glazed). This type of peel is crystallized in sugar.

Pine nuts. The nuts of various pine trees native to China, Italy, Mexico, North Africa and southwestern United States. A shell covers the ivory-colored meat, which is very rich tasting and high in fat. There are two principal types of pine nut — one mild and long-shaped, the other stronger-flavored and more triangular in shape. Substitute for any variety of nut in bread machine recipes.

Pistachio. Inside a hard, tan-colored shell, this pale green nut has a waxy texture and mild flavor.

Pita. A flatbread leavened with yeast to create a hollow center — or "pocket." Middle Eastern pitas tend to be oval while the Greek type are rounder in shape.

Poppy seeds. The tiny, round, blue-gray seed of the poppy has a sweet, nutty flavor. Often used as a garnish or topping for a variety of breads.

Potato starch. This very fine powder is a pure starch made from cooked, dried, ground potatoes. It is gluten-free and produces a moist crumb in baked goods. Potato flour can not be substituted.

Pumpkin seeds. Hulled and roasted pumpkin seeds have a nutty flavor that enhances many breads. In Mexico, they are also known as *pepitas*, where they are eaten as a snack and used as a thickener in cooking.

Quinoa. Pronounced "keen-wa", this was called the "Mother grain" by the ancient Incas. It is a complete protein, containing all 8 essential amino acids. As a grain, it is cooked like rice — although in half the time — and expands to 4 times its original volume. Quinoa is also available ground into flour.

Raisins. Dark raisins are sun-dried Thompson seedless grapes. Golden raisins are treated with sulphur dioxide and dried artificially, yielding a moister, plumper product.

Red River cereal. Originating in the Red River Valley (in Manitoba, Canada), its nutty flavor and chewy texture comes from the combination of cracked wheat, rye and flaxseed.

Rice flour. A fine, powdery-textured flour, gluten-free, it is made from white or brown rice.

Rye flour. Milled from rye, a cereal grain similar to wheat, this flour can be dark or light in color. Because of its low gluten content, it is always used in combination with wheat flour in bread machine recipes.

Rye groat. A rye kernel that has had its husk removed.

Semolina flour. A creamy-yellow, coarsely ground flour milled from hard Durum wheat. It has a high gluten content. Semolina is used either alone or in combination with all-purpose or bread flour to make pasta. The semolina makes it easier to knead and hold its shape during cooking. Sprinkled on a baking sheet, it gives a crunch to Kaisers, French sticks and focaccia.

Sesame seeds. Small, flat, oval-shaped seeds with a rich, nut-like flavor when roasted. Purchase the tan (hulled), not black (unhulled) variety for use in a bread machine.

Shortening. A partially hydrogenated fat made from either animal or vegetable sources.

Nonfat dry milk. The dehydrated form of fluid skim milk. Use 1/4 cup (50 mL) nonfat dry milk for every 1 cup (250 mL) water.

Sour. The "mother" or starter used to ferment the dough for sourdough breads.

Soya flour. Made from toasted soybeans, high in fat and protein. This low-fat flour is milled from raw beans.

Soy flour. Coarser in texture and stronger flavored than soya flour. Gluten-free and not very pleasant tasting, it must be used in combination with other flours.

Spelt. An ancient cereal grain native to Southern Europe, spelt is similar to wheat. The nutty-flavored flour is easily digested and slightly higher in protein than wheat. Use in equal amounts to replace wheat flour. Often is tolerated by those sensitive to wheat flour.

Stone-ground flour. Produced by milling grain between two huge stones without separating the germ. It tends to be a coarser grind than other types of flour.

Sugar substitute. For baking, the best choice is sucralose, which is made from processed sugar, and remains stable at any temperature.

Sun-dried tomatoes. Available either dry or oil-packed, sun-dried tomatoes have a dark red color, soft, chewy texture and strong tomato flavor. Use dry-packed, soft sun-dried tomatoes in bread recipes. If only oil-packed are available, rinse under hot water and dry well before using. Use scissors to snip into pieces.

Sunflower oil. A pale-yellow, flavorless oil, high in polyunsaturated fats and low in saturated fats.

Sunflower seeds. Use shelled, unsalted, unroasted sunflower seeds in bread machine recipes. If only roasted, salted seeds are available, rinse under hot water and dry well before using.

Sweet potato. A tuber with orange flesh that stays moist when cooked. Not the same as a yam, although yams can substitute for sweet potatoes in bread machine recipes.

Tapioca starch. Produced from the root of cassava plant, this starch is used for thickening. Tapioca flour can be substituted.

Tarragon. A herb with narrow, pointed, dark green leaves and a distinctive anise-like flavor with undertones of sage. Use fresh or dried.

Unbleached flour. Gives loaves a creamier color; may be used interchangeably with bleached bread flour.

Vegetable oil. Common oils used are corn, sunflower, safflower, olive, canola, peanut and soya.

Walnuts. A sweet-fleshed nut with a large, wrinkled shell.

Wash. A liquid applied to the surface of risen dough before baking, frequently made from milk, water, or egg.

Webbing. The texture created by holes in artisan, rustic-type breads – usually very large and irregular.

Wheat berry. The berry is the whole wheat kernel which includes the endosperm, bran and germ.

Wheat-blend flour. A blend of flours. May contain cracked wheat, cracked rye, whole flax and wheat bran.

Wheat bran. The outer layer of the wheat berry or kernel, high in fiber and used as a cereal. Oat bran can be substituted in equal amounts.

Wheat germ. The embryo of the wheat berry, wheat germ has a nutty flavor and is rich in vitamins (particularly vitamin E) and minerals. It is oily and must be kept in the refrigerator to prevent it becoming rancid. Wheat germ cannot be substituted for wheat bran.

White flour. A flour made by finely grinding the wheat kernel and separating out the germ and bran. It is enriched with vitamins (thiamine, niacin, riboflavin, folic acid) and minerals (iron).

Whole-wheat flour. A flour made by grinding the entire wheat berry – the bran, germ and endosperm. Store in freezer to keep fresh.

Wild rice. Native to North America, this nutty-flavored seed does not come from a rice plant, but from a type of grass.

Xanthan gum. Used as an ingredient in gluten-free bread to give the dough strength, thus allowing it to rise and prevent it from being too dense in texture. It does not mix with water, so must be combined with dry ingredients. Purchase from bulk or health-food stores.

Yeast. A tiny, single-celled organism that, given moisture, food and warmth, creates gas that is trapped in bread dough, causing it to rise.

Yogurt. Made by fermenting cows' milk using a bacteria culture.

Zest. Strips from the outer layer of rind of citrus fruit. Used for its intense flavor.

Techniques Glossary

Almonds. *To blanch:* Cover almonds with boiling water and allow to stand, covered, for 3 to 5 minutes; drain. Grasp the almond at one end, pressing between your thumb and index finger and the nut will pop out of the skin. Nuts are more easily chopped or slivered while still warm from blanching. *To toast:* see Nuts.

Bananas. *To mash and freeze:* Select overripe fruit, mash and package in 1-cup (250 mL) amounts in freezer containers. Freeze for up to 6 months. Defrost and warm to room temperature before using.

Bagel chips. *To make:* Cut bagels in half to form 2 half-circles, then slice 1/8 inch (2 mm) thick. Brush with olive oil and bake at 400° F (200° C) for 12 minutes or until crisp.

Chocolate. *To melt:* Foods high in fat (such as chocolate) soften and then become a liquid when heated. Microwave on High for 1 minute per 1-oz (30 g) square.

Coconut. *To toast:* see Oats.

Cups. See Roasted vegetable cups.

Danish. See Fun shapes.

Doubled in Volume. See Proof.

Drizzle. To slowly spoon or pour a liquid (such as icing or melted butter) in a very fine stream over food.

Dust. To coat by sprinkling confectioner's sugar, cocoa or flour lightly over food or a utensil.

Flaxseed. *To grind:* Place whole seeds in a coffee grinder or blender. Grind only the amount required. If necessary, store extra ground flaxseed in refrigerator.

Freezing dough. Seal dough in airtight containers and freeze for up to 4 weeks. Thaw, wrapped, overnight in the refrigerator. *Refrigerating dough:* 1 to 2 hours after dough is refrigerated, dough must be punched down, then punched down every 24 hours. For best results, use within 48 hours.

Fun shapes. To make *snails*, coil rope of dough tightly; instead of tucking end under, raise it, and flatten to form ears and head. This can quickly and easily be changed to a *rattlesnake* by raising the center tail. *Cats*, *squirrels* and *bunnies* can be made by cutting off 2- to 3- inch (5 to 9.5 cm) pieces for ears and a tail. A double coil in 2:1 or 2:3 proportion shaped into a figure "8" forms the head and the body.

Garlic. *To roast:* Cut off top of head to expose clove tips. Drizzle with 1/4 tsp (1 mL) olive oil and microwave on High for 70 seconds or until fork tender. (Or bake at 375° F [190° C] for 15 to 20 minutes.) *To peel:* Use the flat side of a sharp knife to flatten the clove of garlic. Then the skin can be easily removed.

Glaze. To apply a thin, shiny coating to the outside of a sweet or savory food.

Hazelnuts. *To remove skins:* Place hazelnuts in a 350° F (180° C) oven for 15 to 20 minutes. Immediately place in a clean, dry kitchen towel. With your hands, rub the nuts against the towel. (Skins will be left in the towel. Be careful: hazelnuts will be very hot).

Nuts. *To toast:* Spread nuts in a single layer on a baking sheet and bake at 350° F (180° C) for about 10 minutes, shaking the pan frequently, until lightly browned. (Or microwave uncovered on High for 1 to 2 minutes, stirring every 30 seconds.) Nuts will darken upon cooling.

Oats. *To toast:* Spread rolled oats in a shallow pan. Bake at 350° F (180° C) for 10 to 15 minutes or until brown; stir often. Store in an airtight container or freeze.

Olives. *To pit:* Place olives under the flat side of a large knife; push down on knife until pit pops out.

Onions. *To caramelize:* In a nonstick frying pan, heat 1 tbsp (15 mL) oil over medium heat. Add 2 cups (500 mL) sliced or chopped onions; cook slowly until soft and caramel-colored. If necessary, add 1 tbsp (15 mL) water or white wine to prevent sticking while cooking.

Pita. *To heat:* Place pita(s) on baking sheet and bake in preheated oven 400° F (200° C) for about 8 minutes. For a softer sandwich, wrap in foil before heating. To microwave, place on a plate lined with paper towels and heat on High for 1 to 2 minutes. *To make pita chips or crisps:* Separate the layers of the pita by cutting or pulling apart. Cut both circles into 4 or 8 wedges, depending on the size of the pita. Bake, turning once in a 350° F (180° C) oven for 10 to 15 minutes or until lightly browned and crisp (or broil for 2 to 4 minutes until golden and crisp).

Proof. The period of time during which shaped yeast products rise before baking. Poke dough with two fingers. When indents remain, dough has doubled in volume.

Roasted vegetable cups. *To make:* Line the cups of muffin tins with 3-inch (7.5 cm) circles of dough. Fill each with roasted vegetables. Bake in a 350° F (180° C) oven for 15 to 20 minutes or until heated through.

Rye groats. *To cook:* Cover with at least 1 inch (2.5 cm) water and let stand overnight. Drain. Add fresh water to cover. Simmer, stirring occasionally, for 20 to 30 minutes or until tender. Drain and allow to cool before using. Store in refrigerator.

Sauté. To cook quickly in a small amount of fat at a high temperature.

Shaping a loaf for a loaf pan. Roll out the dough into an 11- by 8-inch (27.5 by 20 cm) rectangle. Roll up, beginning at the long side, pinching the seam to seal. Tuck under ends. Place in loaf pan, seam-side down.

Slash. This allows for the expansion of bread while baking. Hold *lame* or sharp knife at a 45° angle. Quickly cut the top of the dough in one long motion. The cuts must be at least 1/4 to 1/2 inch (0.5 to 2 mm) deep. The deeper the cut, the more open the slash.

Spritz. To spray risen dough with water before and during baking for a crisp crust.

Steaming. Preheat fire bricks or lava rocks in a 9- by 13-inch (3 L) metal baking pan. Place the dough in oven. Quickly add 1 cup (250 mL) of cold water to the pan of bricks. Close the door quickly to prevent the steam from escaping. Alternatively, spray the dough with a fine mist of cold water. The spray should not touch the oven sides, back or floor. Repeat in 30 seconds and again 2 to 3 times during the next 3 minutes. You can also place a 9- by 13-inch (3 L) metal baking pan in the oven while it is preheating. Add a tray of ice cubes to the preheated pan, then quickly close the oven door.

Vegetables. *To sweat:* In a pan over low heat, cook vegetables, covered, in a small amount of fat. The food softens and releases water. This allows the flavors to release quickly when cooked with another food.

Wheat berry. *To cook:* In a bowl cover wheat berry with at least 1 inch (2.5 cm) water; let stand overnight. Drain. Add fresh water to cover. Transfer to a pot over medium heat. Simmer, stirring occasionally, for 30 to 45 minutes or until tender. Drain and allow to cool before using. Store in refrigerator.

Wild rice. *To cook:* For each 1 cup (250 mL) wild rice, add 2 cups (500 mL) water to a large saucepan. Cover and simmer for 40 to 50 minutes or until rice is tender and splitting. Drain well. Store in refrigerator.

Zest. *To zest:* Use a zester or small sharp knife to peel off thin strips of the colored part of the skin. Be sure not to remove the bitter white pith below.

Index

A

Almond paste:
 filling, 98-99
 to soften, 98
Almond(s):
 apricot yogurt bread, 73
 Baltic bread, 118-19
 finish, 118-19
 spelt bread, 158
 topping, 160-61
 to toast, 183
Amaranth:
 ancient grains bread, 154
 granary bread, 31
Amish seed bread, 74
Ancient grains bread, 154
Apple(s):
 blueberry streusel cake, 102-3
 fruited pumpernickel, 18-19
 jelly, 174
 yam loaf, 13
 yield, shredded, 13
Applesauce:
 cinnamon oat bread, 20
 whole wheat loaf, 97
Après ski loaf, 60
Apricot(s):
 almond yogurt bread, 73
 filling, 160-61
 fruited pumpernickel, 18-19
 tea ring, 160-61
Asiago cheese, herb loaf, 14
Autumn pumpkin loaf, 100-101

B

Baba au orange, 116-17
Baba au rhum, 116-17
Bacon, mock spoon bread, 33
Bagel(s):
 basic, 85
 chips, 183
 cinnamon raisin, 86
 multigrain, 87
 tips, 84

Baguettes, 60
 multi-seed, 64
 pans, 176
 sourdough, 93
Baltic birthday bread, 118-19
Banana(s):
 maple flaxseed loaf, 78-79
 peanut butter swirl loaf, 137
 quick bread, 169
 to freeze, 78
Barley flakes:
 après ski loaf, 60
 brown seed bread, 75
 granary bread, 31
Bars:
 Nanaimo, 111
 oatmeal raisin, 172
Basic bagels, 85
Basic fresh pasta, 165
Basic sour mix, 89
Beer, pretzels, 148
Blueberry(ies):
 peach streusel cake, 102-3
 poppy loaf, 104
 to freeze, 102
 and wild rice loaf, 39
Boule, sourdough, 94
Braids:
 cheese, 54-55
 circle of light, 136
 squash crescent, 61
 Ukrainian egg bread, 126-27
Bran cereal:
 brown seed bread, 75
 carrot bread, 159
 raisin bran loaf, 36
Bread machines, sizes and capacities, 8
Breadsticks, twisted, 68
Brown seed bread, 75
Buckwheat flour, granary bread, 31
Bulgur crown, 69
Bundles:
 date orange, 106-7
 kolach, 123

Buns:
  sourdough hamburger, 92
  sticky, 152-53
Buttermilk powder:
  breadsticks, 68
  carrot bran bread, 159
  cheese braid, 54-55
  honey berry seed bread, 76
  kaffeekuchen, 120-21
  muffaletta, 44-45
  pumpernickel turban, 140-41
  soda bread, 122
  soup-in-a-bread-bowl, 142
  spinach pitas, 43
  toasties, 66-67
  wheat berry crown, 69
Butters, orange honey, 70
Butterscotch chips, pumpkin loaf, 100-101

C

Cakes:
  baking tips, 168
  blueberry peach streusel, 102-3
  lemon, 170
  orange glazed breakfast, 112
  pineapple coconut, 171
California garlic with sun-dried tomatoes, 15
Calzones, stuffed with roasted vegetables,
    48-49
Caraway rye bread, 29
Carrot pineapple bread, 16
Cheddar cheese:
  braid, turkey-filled, 54-55
  lavosh, 52-53
  mock spoon bread, 33
  potato loaf, 17
  sourdough hamburger buns, 92
Cheesecake, raspberry, 173
Cheesy potato loaf, 17
Chocolate:
  hazelnut bread, 110
  raspberry Danish, 131
  Valentine bread, 146-47
Chocolate chips, Nanaimo bar loaf, 111
Christine's fruited pumpernickel, 18-19
Christmas cranberry Kringle, 98-99
Ciabatta, 56

Cinnamon:
  apple oat bread, 20
  filling, 138-39
  raisin bagels, 86
Circles:
  Christmas cranberry Kringle, 98-99
  kolaches, 123, 126-27
  of light, 136
Cloverleaf rolls, 63
Cocoa:
  chocolate hazelnut bread, 110
  java crunch loaf, 77
  Nanaimo bar loaf, 111
Coconut:
  Hawaiian sweet bread, 109
  Nanaimo bar loaf, 111
  pineapple cake, 171
  to toast, 183
Coffee:
  chocolate crunch loaf, 77
  pumpernickel turban, 140-41
Coffeecake, 120-21
Cookies:
  baking tips, 168
  oatmeal raisin, 172
Corn, mock spoon bread, 33
Cornmeal:
  ancient grains bread, 154
  mock spoon bread, 33
  Moroccan anise bread, 47
  San Francisco Firehouse bread, 26
  sesame bread, 37
  spelt bread, 158
Cottage cheese:
  brown seed bread, 75
  orange glazed breakfast cake, 112
Cracked wheat:
  après ski loaf, 60
  baguettes, 64
  double-crunch bread, 30
  rolls, 59
  soup-in-a-bread-bowl, 142
  triple-wheat bread, 38
Cranberry(ies):
  Christmas Kringle, 98
  filling, 120-21
  pumpkin loaf, 100-101
  raisin loaf, 108

Cranberry(ies), continued:
  walnut kaffeekuchen, 120-21
  and wild rice loaf, 39
Cream cheese:
  and pear filling, 146-47
  raspberry cheesecake, 173
Crisps, pecan, 138-39
Croutons, 25
Cumin rye bread, 29
Currants, granola loaf, 32

D

Daffodil bread, 105
Danishes, chocolate raspberry, 131
Date(s):
  bran loaf, 36
  carrot bran bread, 159
  filling, 106-7
  fruited pumpernickel, 18-19
  orange bundles, 106-7
Double-crunch wheat bread, 30
Dried cranberry *See* Cranberry

E

Egg white, glaze, 106-7
Egg yolk, glaze, 50-51, 65, 98-99
English muffins:
  loaf, 21
  whole wheat, 70

F

Fats, 10
Feta cheese, Mediterranean bread, 124
Fettuccine, 166
Figs, fruited pumpernickel, 18-19
Fillings:
  apricot, 160-61
  cinnamon, 138-39
  cranberry, 120-21
  mincemeat, 123
  peanut butter, 137
  pear and cream cheese, 146-47
  tips for preparing, 42
  turkey, 54-55
Finishes:
  almond, 118-19
  oatmeal, 115
Flatbread, 47

Flaxseed:
  to grind, 183
  low-fat bread, 156-57
  maple banana loaf, 78-79
  spelt bread, 158
  triple-wheat bread, 38
Flour, and gluten, 9
Focaccia, red onion, 46
Friendly Frosty, 134-35
Fruit, pumpernickel, 18-19
Fruit peel, Baltic bread, 118-19
Fun shapes:
  Frosty, 134-35
  piggies, 132-33
  sunflower, 144-45
  tips, 130

G

Garlic:
  with sun-dried tomato bread, 15
  to roast, 183
German lentil soup, 143
Glaze:
  egg white, 106-7
  egg yolk, 50-51, 65, 98-99
  lemon, 112
  orange, 112, 144-45
  pecan pan, 152-53
  seed, 61, 64
Gluten-free breads:
  pumpernickel loaf, 151
  sticky buns, 152-53
  tips for baking, 150
Grains, tips for, 28
Granary bread, 31
Granola currant loaf, 32

H

Ham, mock spoon bread, 33
Hamburger buns, sourdough, 92
Hawaiian sunrise bread, 109
Hazelnut(s):
  chocolate bread, 110
  to remove skins, 183
Hearth breads:
  steps to preparing, 58
Herbs:
  Asiago loaf, 14

Herbs (continued):
poultry-stuffing loaf, 25
San Francisco Firehouse bread, 26
tomato pasta, 167
High-fiber breads:
almond apricot yogurt, 73
Amish seed, 74
carrot bran, 159
maple banana flaxseed, 78
Honey, berry seed bread, 76

I

Ingredients, temperature of, 9
Irish barm bran bread, 115
Irish freckle bread, 122

J

Jams:
strawberry rhubarb, 175
tips for making, 174
Java chocolate crunch loaf, 77
Jelly:
apple, 174
tips for making, 174

K

Kamut:
ancient grains bread, 154
granary bread, 31
Kolaches, 123, 126-27
bundles, 123
Kuchen, radar, 125

L

Lavosh, sun-dried tomato, 52-53
Leeks, and mushroom bread, 23
Lemon:
cake, 170
daffodil bread, 105
glaze, 112
syrup, 170
Lentil soup, 143
Liquids, 9
Low-fat bread, flaxseed, 156-57

M

Malt syrup, rye bread, 22
Maple syrup:
banana flaxseed bread, 78-79

Maple syrup (continued):
walnut loaf, 62
Mediterranean bread, 124
Mincemeat filling, 123
Mock spoon bread, 33
Moroccan anise bread, 47
Muesli raisin loaf, 32
Muffaletta, New Orleans-style, 44-45
Multigrain bagels, 87
Multi-seed baguettes, 64
Mushroom leek bread, 23

N

Nanaimo bar loaf, 111
New England maple leaf walnut loaf, 62
New Orleans-style muffaletta, 44-45
Nuts, fat/fiber connection, 72

O

Oat bran:
cinnamon apple bread, 20
raisin loaf, 36
Oatmeal:
après ski loaf, 60
finish, 115
raisin bars, 172
Oats:
Amish seed bread, 74
cinnamon apple bread, 20
granary bread, 31
Irish barm bread, 115
oatmeal raisin bars, 172
Old-fashioned wheat bread, 34
Olives, Mediterranean bread, 124
Onion Cheddar sourdough hamburger buns, 92
Onion flakes, rye loaf, 35
Orange:
daffodil bread, 105
date bundles, 106-7
glaze, 144-45
glazed breakfast cake, 112
honey butter, 70

P

Pan rolls, 59
Parmesan cheese:
braid, 54-55
lavosh, 52-53
pesto loaf, 24

Pasta:
  cooking fresh, 166
  tips for making, 164
  tomato-herb, 167
Pasta flour:
  pasta, 165
  sesame bread, 37
Peach, blueberry streusel cake, 102-3
Peanut butter:
  banana swirl loaf, 137
  filling, 137
  rye loaf, 80
Peanuts:
  rye loaf, 80
  wild rice and cranberry loaf, 39
Pear, and cream cheese filling, 146-47
Pecans:
  braided crescent, 61
  crisps, 138-39
  Nanaimo bar loaf, 111
  pan glaze, 152-53
  topping, 138-39
Pesto loaf, 24
Pesto sauce, about, 24
Piggies, 132-33
Pineapple:
  carrot bread, 16
  coconut cake, 171
  sweet bread, 109
Pine nuts:
  pesto loaf, 24
  wild rice and cranberry loaf, 39
Pistachio nuts, coffee chocolate loaf, 77
Pitas, spinach, 43
Poppy seeds:
  blueberry loaf, 104
  thyme loaf, 81
Potatoes, cloverleaf rolls, 63
Potato flakes, cheesy loaf, 17
Potato starch:
  pumpernickel loaf, 151
  sticky buns, 152-53
Poultry-stuffing loaf, 25
Pretzels, soft, 148
Prunes, fruited pumpernickel, 18-19
Pumpernickel:
  fruited bread, 18-19
  turban, 140-41
Pumpkin, loaf, 100-101

Q
Quick breads, banana, 169
Quick-cooking oats. *See* Oats
Quick low-fat honey flaxseed bread, 156-57
Quick poultry-stuffing loaf, 25
Quinoa:
  ancient grains bread, 154
  granary bread, 31

R
Radar kuchen, 125
Raisin(s):
  Baltic bread, 118-19
  bran loaf, 36
  cinnamon bagels, 86
  cranberry loaf, 108
  Muesli loaf, 32
  oatmeal bars, 172
  soda bread, 122
  walnut sourdough, 91
  whole wheat applesauce loaf, 97
Rapid cycles, using, 155
Raspberry:
  cheesecake, 173
  chocolate Danishes, 131
Red onion focaccia, 46
Red River cereal, multigrain bagels, 87
Rhubarb, and strawberry jam, 175
Rice flour:
  pumpernickel loaf, 151
  sticky buns, 152-53
Roasted vegetables:
  filling, 48-49
  -stuffed calzones, 48-49
Rolls:
  cloverleaf, 63
  Irish barm, 115
  pan, 59
  sour cream pansies, 65
  steps to preparing, 58
  12-grain, 59
Rum syrup, baba, 116-17
Rye berries, crown, 69
Rye flakes, après ski loaf, 60
Rye flour:
  cumin bread, 29
  fruited pumpernickel, 18-19
  malted rye bread, 22
  onion loaf, 35

Rye flour (continued):
  peanut loaf, 80
  pumpernickel turban, 140-41
  sourdough boule, 94
  Swiss rye loaf, 128
Rye groats:
  granary bread, 31
  Swiss rye loaf, 128
  to cook, 184

S
Saffron threads, Baltic bread, 118-19
Salt, 9
Sandwiches:
  focaccia, 46
  piggies, 132-33
  Tuscan walnut toasties, 66-67
San Francisco Firehouse bread, 26
Sausage-stuffed stromboli, 50-51
Seed(s):
  baguettes, 64
  brown bread, 75
  fat/fiber connection, 72
  glaze, 61, 64
  honey berry bread, 76
  and soy loaf, 162
  topping, 140-41
Semolina:
  ancient grains bread, 154
  fresh pasta, 165
  sesame bread, 37
  spinach pasta, 166
  tomato-herb pasta, 167
Sesame seeds:
  Amish bread, 74
  semolina bread, 37
7-grain cereal:
  muffaletta, 44-45
  multigrain bagels, 87
Shapes. See Fun shapes
Soda bread, Irish, 122
Soup:
  -in-a-bread-bowl, 142
  lentil, 143
Sour cherries, and wild rice loaf, 39
Sour cream:
  blueberry poppy loaf, 104
  pansies, 65

Sourdough:
  baguettes, 93
  basic mix, 89
  boule, 94
  French walnut raisin, 91
  onion Cheddar hamburger buns, 92
  starters vs. sours, 88
  tips for working with, 90
Soy flour, and seed loaf, 162
Spaghetti, 165
Spelt:
  ancient grains bread, 154
  bread, 158
  granary bread, 31
Spinach:
  pasta, 166
  pitas, 43
Squash, braided crescent, 61
Steaming, instructions, 184
Sticky buns, 152-53
Strawberry rhubarb jam, 175
Streusel topping, 102-3
Stromboli, sausage-stuffed, 50-51
Sugar-free:
  apricot tea ring, 160-61
  Moroccan anise bread, 47
  Swiss rye, 128
Sugars, 10
Sugar substitutes, 181
Summer sunflower, 144-45
Sun-dried tomatoes:
  with garlic bread, 15
  herb pasta, 167
  lavosh, 52-53
  rosemary ciabatta, 56
Sunflower seeds:
  après ski loaf, 60
  double-crunch wheat bread, 30
  summer sunflower, 144-45
  wheat berry crown, 69
  wild rice and cranberry loaf, 39
Sweet breads, 109
  birthday, 118-19
  cranberry walnut kaffeekuchen, 120-21
  hazelnut chocolate, 110
  tips for making, 96
Swiss rye loaf, 128
Syrup, lemon, 170
  See also Maple syrup

T

Tapioca starch:
  pumpernickel loaf, 151
  sticky buns, 152-53
Testing for doneness, 9
Thanksgiving, circle of light, 136
Three little piggies, 132-33
Thyme, poppy loaf, 81
Toasties, Tuscan walnut, 66-67
Tomatoes. *See* Sun-dried tomatoes
Toppings:
  almond, 160-61
  pecan, 138-39
  pretzel, 148
  seed, 140-41
  streusel, 102-3
  sunflower seed, 144-45
  walnut, 120-21
Trail mix, bread, 82
Triple-wheat bread, 38
Turban, pumpernickel, 140-41
Turkey-filled cheese braid, 54-55
Tuscan walnut toasties, 66-67
12-grain cereal, rolls, 59
Twists:
  breadsticks, 68
  radar, 125

U

Ukrainian egg bread, 126-27

V

Valentine chocolate sweetheart bread, 146-47
Vegetables, to sweat, 184

W

Walnuts:
  maple loaf, 62
  raisin sourdough, 91
  toasties, 66-67
  topping, 120-21
Wheat berries:
  crown, 69
  honey seed bread, 76
  Irish barm bread, 115
  to cook, 184
  triple-wheat bread, 38
Wheat bran:
  Amish seed bread, 74

Wheat bran (continued):
  Irish barm bread, 115
  raisin bran loaf, 36
  and yogurt bread, 40
Wheat germ:
  multigrain bagels, 87
  rolls, 59
  and yogurt bread, 40
Whole wheat:
  Amish seed bread, 74
  applesauce loaf, 97
  baguettes, 64
  carrot bran bread, 159
  ciabatta, 56
  English muffins, 70
  honey berry seed bread, 76
  Irish barm bread, 115
  malted rye bread, 22
  maple banana flaxseed loaf, 78-79
  Moroccan anise bread, 47
  muffaletta, 44-45
  multigrain bagels, 87
  mushroom leek bread, 23
  old-fashioned bread, 34
  piggies, 132-33
  pumpernickel turban, 140-41
  raisin bran loaf, 36
  rolls, 59
  San Francisco Firehouse bread, 26
  seed and soy loaf, 162
  soup-in-a-bread-bowl, 142
  spinach pitas, 43
  Swiss rye loaf, 128
  triple-wheat bread, 38
  walnut raisin sourdough, 91
  wheat berry crown, 69
  and yogurt bread, 40
Wild rice and cranberry loaf, 39

Y

Yam, apple loaf, 13
Yeast, 10
Yogurt:
  almond apricot bread, 73
  Amish seed bread, 74
  Irish barm bran bread, 115
  raspberry cheesecake, 173
  trail mix bread, 82
  wheat-germ bread, 40

EVEN MORE BREAD!

Now you can get even more great bread machine recipes by subscribing to Donna and Heather's newsletter, *The Bread Basket*. Published by Quality Professional Services (QPS) and written specially for bread machine owners, this bimonthly publication features 12 pages of useful information, including:

- Seven previously unpublished bread machine recipes — with quantities for both 1.5 and 2 lb machines (even some for 1 lb and 2.5 lb models) — from the QPS test kitchen

- Tips on buying and using different types of flours, grains and other ingredients

- What you need to know about the features of various bread machines in order to make an informed purchase decision

- Answers to readers' questions

- And much, much more...

Annual subscriptions cost only $16.00. Send your cheque, payable to Quality Professional Services, to:

QPS
P. O. Box 1781
Ogdensburg, NY 13669

For more information, call
(613) 923-2116
or visit our website at
www.bestbreadrecipes.com

Be sure to include your name, address and zip code.

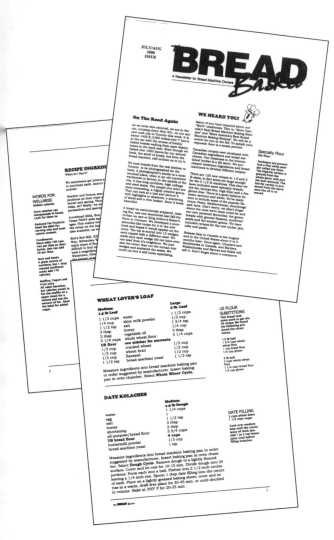